Feng Shui For The
Real Estate Agent
(and The Homeowner, Too!)

Feng Shui For The Real Estate Agent

(and The Homeowner, Too!)

Steve Kodad

Real Estate Broker and
Feng Shui Practitioner

CONTENTS

INTRODUCTION

A funny thing happened on my way out the door one day. I was attempting to check my e-mail rather quickly, and get to the office for what looked like another long day. I have the habit of automatically deleting most of the e-mail messages I get without ever opening them, but this day one of them jumped out at me. It was certainly an advertisement, but it seemed to be directed at me personally. This tantalizing subject line was stating that there was a way to sell my listings quicker and possibly for more money. For a real estate agent, this kind of content is like waving a piece of meat in front of a dog that hasn't eaten in three days. So I decided I'd pull up this little advertisement and risk being late for my office appointment. The ad was about a topic I knew very little about . . . Feng Shui! Like more than half of the United States, I had heard it might make my environment better, but it what way? Many people have never heard of it, and most could not pronounce it correctly either!

Well, I knew I had to get back in to the real world and keep my appointment, but I kept thinking about this e-mail throughout the day. What if it was true? What if, by simply performing something called Feng Shui on my listings, I could be more successful? What if I could actually do something that was successful, but also something that set me apart from the thousands and thousands of other real estate agents in this country? Any salesman is always hoping to be different. As a real estate agent who has been licensed in three states, I have certainly tried many of the "new" strategies to attract customers to my door step. All of these strategies seemed to have the same promise—more customers, more closings, and less work. We are all looking for that "magic" pill. We all hope that something like this exists, because sales can be a very humbling vocation. But most of us know it's a long shot.

The scary thing for any salesman is that no matter how good a month or year you have, the calendar turns and you have to do it all over again. Many questions crop up on the 1st of every month and the 1st of every year. *Can*

I do it again? What if my clients dry up? Can I meet my advertising bills this month? Will I have to take a second job? For many of us, the last question is really scary!!! Let me say this right away, selling real estate is not easy. Many "outsiders" think that an agent makes tons of money for doing very little work. Agents know this is a total fallacy. First, an agent has to sift through many dead ends and potential customers who waste time by "kicking tires" just to find a customer or two. Those "good" customers may look at 20 to 30 homes before actually getting to the closing table.

Even when a home buyer has finally found "the right one", things can and often do go wrong. Inspections, appraisals, and credit problems are just a few of the many things a real estate agent has to deal with. It is very true that an agent who is totally committed to making real estate his or her way of making a living is always "on call", and often has trouble getting away. As a result, there is a lot of burn-out in this profession. Many new agents never even get to their second or third year. Home sellers often feel that calling their agent after 9 PM is part of the job description. Every agent loves those frantic calls, late at night, stating that the flyer box is empty . . . and how soon will it be re-filled?

Listing, marketing, and selling a home are totally different aspects of being a real estate agent, and sometimes take up more of an agent's time than the actual sell. A homeowner demands certain things from the agent, but the primary demand is that the agent get the house sold as quickly as possible and for a good price. This is the classic "hero" or "bum" scenario. You can be a complete screw-up most of the time, but if an agent brings you and your seller an acceptable offer fairly quickly . . . "you da man"! But on the other side, you may be absolutely outstanding in all of your efforts for 90 days or more, but not get the home under contract . . . suddenly, you are the "worst agent ever"! And emotions and tags can change rather quickly. Conclusion: an agent is only as good as the results at any given moment.

The life of the real estate agent has gotten more and more complicated. Agents are expected to keep up with the latest technology, but still offer that "old time service". Often they are expected to juggle several tasks at one time . . . but never let them see you sweat! A relationship with a buyer or a seller can become very close, is sometimes very heated, and often extends over a period of months. The expectations are high, but the reward can also be high!

Today, an agent can expect to be contacted many times during a day. There was a time when it was harder to get you, but with the advent of the cell phone . . . no time or place is a deterrent for a determined client. Let's hear it for the cell phone! Anyone out there ever go on a date with their significant other, only to get an urgent phone call from a seller complaining about the lights being left on after an afternoon showing?

There are many, many more people in real estate today. They, like some of your clients, thought it was easy money, then reality set in, and the usual 25% to 30% of the work force turned over. This happens every year. I'm sure you have known an eager agent or two (or twelve) who was sure he would "set the world on fire", but ended up disillusioned and sadly looking for a "real job" after a few months. Wouldn't it be nice to get some consistency in your life? Wouldn't it be amazing to find a niche that would enable you to offer something different—some thing that distinguishes you from the thousands of real estate agents who have learned the "how we always do it" mentality?

The primary focus of this book is to enable you (the real estate agent or the home seller) to get a home sold with less stress, less effort, and more reliability. Each chapter is written to educate you about Feng Shui; one chapter even advises you on ways to deal with the home buyer who is Feng Shui savvy. Surprisingly, more and more buyers want to consider this philosophy in their buying decision. Many people in the United States are discovering the benefits of this ancient philosophy. Many of them have either felt these effects already in their environment or desire them . . . peace, better health, creativity and success.

I believe you will find this book to be a powerful way to incorporate this four thousand year-old philosophy of Feng Shui into getting your homes sold, but I think it will also provide a stimulus for you to become more knowledgeable about the world of Feng Shui. Feng Shui can be a big plus in improving your business and your bottom line, but it also can dramatically change how you look at the world. By the way, Feng Shui is pronounced "Fung Shway". So . . . lesson one . . . repeat after me, 10 times . . . . *Feng Shui!*

*"One can not collect all the beautiful shells on the beach.
One can collect only a few, and they are more beautiful if
they are few"*

Anne Morrow Lindbergh

"Gift From The Sea"
1955

CHAPTER 1

The Evolution of Feng Shui

Feng Shui has been used around the world for thousands of years. Originally, it probably didn't have any particular name; it was just good common sense around camp or in town. Man has always known it is smart to coordinate with Mother Nature. Why fight her? Why not learn to "fit in" with her immense and always changing power? While life was not as complex as it is today, there have always been human beings who noticed what worked in different situations. They made observations and took note.

Hundreds of thousands of years ago, a person had to learn rather quickly that certain locations, certain materials, or certain objects made day-to-day existence easier and more healthful. It also helped to notice that certain locations would open up all sorts of scary possibilities (no, not ridicule . . . that came later!). The world always seemed somewhat out of personal control, so anything that increased one's chances for survival was important to remember. A person didn't know when he left his dwelling in the morning whether he would be bringing home the bacon, or if he would end up being the bacon!

Human beings needed to give some real thought about where they dropped their blankets. All types of consequences could occur if they just picked a pretty view, without considering all the possible outcomes, or if they were feeling a little lazy and didn't want to keep looking for a safer place.

Let's suppose the hero of our story (we'll call him Clarence) picked out a nice little cave that faced north and was four miles from the nearest water. Although the cave was snug and cozy in the summertime, his wife might have gotten just a little tired of the daily trip to the spring and back, and therefore considered leaving Clarence for a smarter guy—one who lived a little closer to water. Or perhaps she instead decided to make the trek every third day—after all, with a little less cleaning and cooking, not nearly as much water was needed.

As you can see, we have the beginnings of some of the earliest marital problems going on here—problems that could have been avoided if Clarence had considered the elements more carefully.

When the cold winds began to blow into their north-facing dwelling during the winter months, pushing up their fueling costs and making their comfort a constant sore subject between them, these things would further upset Jill, and cause her to fake more and more headaches . . . well, you can figure it out. So, you see that a poor selection of a place to call home led to many problems, and eventually destroyed Clarence's chance to keep the family line going.

Prehistoric cave painting, Lascaux France

Location has always been an important consideration for the survival of mankind; many things had to be taken into account before you just pitched your tent or started painting the cave wall. Was there enough game in the area? Was there plenty of clean water? Were the elements harsh or comfortable? Did you feel safe from ferocious animals, including other Clarences? Would your crops get rain and grow consistently?

Our hero (and heroine) needed to take into account many things before settling in, and since these things could change rather quickly, they had to learn to be flexible. They constantly learned what worked and what didn't. They experimented every day with the natural world, made mistakes, and made corrections.

They didn't know it at the time, but they were developing a philosophy about how to live life more successfully . . . a philosophy that still applies to the modern world. In a lot of ways, Clarence wanted less stress in his life, better working conditions, a better relationship with Jill, and peace and harmony in his home and family. Although the world is always changing, man has remained constant in his search for those things . . . things we still crave today.

Through the years, as a species, we have gotten better in controlling our environment. Progress has been slow. Different civilizations died out, and others prospered, but we gradually created ways to live that continue to evolve and improve. Mistakes and corrections formed not only how we moved towards better living conditions, healthier lifestyles or improved farming techniques, but our philosophies of life as well . . . this is certainly how *Feng Shui* developed.

Feng Shui has developed slowly over thousands of years; some say as many as 5,000 years. The philosophy took many turns and some of them were disasters, but out of disasters, change and "ah ha's" happened. *Feng Shui* developed by adjusting to this puzzle we call everyday life. Although many people associate the start of *Feng Shui* with China, some schools feel the start was actually in India, sweeping into Tibet, and finally becoming firmly entrenched in China. Over the years, different schools and philosophies developed in separate locations and have become as one in their main ideas.

15

It began rather simply, with people like Clarence and Jill developing some rules about how the universe worked and how they could live more successful lives. Man took notice of how the seasons were important to crops and when and where to plant, how the stars changed location and what this meant, and they were able to understand the different patterns of existence that surrounded them.

In ancient China, the burial of a beloved ancestor was one of the first uses of this new set of ideas. It was thought if you buried your loved ones in a safe, positive environment protected from the elements, and provided them a nice, panoramic view, these ancestors would watch over you from the afterlife, ease your burdens, and make your life on earth more successful.

The cultivation of crops also took on a whole new meaning by making sure they were planted at the most opportune time, place, and direction.

Of course the rulers of this time made sure that most of the "good stuff" was kept secret from the masses. After all, they didn't want the workers to get too successful! So for a good while—try hundreds and hundreds of years—the big-shots made sure that they planned their lives and built their new mansions and temples according to powerful *Feng Shui* principles known only to themselves and their trusted *Feng Shui* masters. The "secrets" and principles of *Feng Shui* were passed on from Master to the next generation Master. But it became increasingly more difficult to keep secrets, and these ideas started to slip out to the common people. During imperial times it was possible for people to actually sue another for infringing the rules of good *Feng Shui*.

Over time, these ideas were recorded in a book called the **"I Ching"**, frequently called the "Book of Changes". This book was the formalization of a lot of the ideas and terminology still used today. *Feng Shui* practitioners around the world still look for guidance and direction from this ancient text.

During the Zhou dynasty (1046-256 BC), an early text talked about a person known as Gong Liu who seemed to conduct an early type of *Feng Shui* analysis on the land. The excerpt stated that Gong Liu

". . . surveyed the breadth and length of his lands; he measured the shadow and observed the hills, noting the sunshine and shade. He located the streams and springs . . .".

What is interesting about this passage is that *sunshine* and *shade* are the original meanings of the well-known terms you will hear frequently in this book, *Yin* and *Yang*.

Feng Shui, which literally means "Wind" and "Water", began to become more formalized in southwest China, with its dramatic, pronounced topology of jutting mountains and plentiful water features. This topology led ancient experts to look at the **Form** or **Land Form**. This is our first school of *Feng Shui*. This led to the ideal site for building . . . the "armchair" location. Simply, a *Feng Shui* practitioner at this time was looking for a mountain behind for optimal protection against the elements, and possibly, other humans. Stability behind your structure would give you both physical and mental safety. On the sides, the arms of the chair needed to offer protection too. A grove of trees or a hill was important to cut down the wind and give gentle breezes, and offer a milder climate. The front view was also very important. It needed to offer a wide view of the country to have ample warning of unwanted visitors. Hopefully a body of water would also contribute to a pleasing view. It was even more auspicious if the north was behind and the south was in front. This offered a milder winter, and a good place to grow the crops.

Directions became a very important part of the puzzle for anyone wanting the environment to be aligned perfectly for success and good health. Confucius was inspired by the idea that perfect government reflected great harmony between leaders and inhabitants, and yearned for the creation of perfection in humans and the environment in which they lived.

Of course, all locations on Earth do not offer this particular type of topology, and other geographic areas of the world had to look at their areas quite differently; as a result they developed a slightly different philosophy of their environment. The inhabitants of northern China had to consider a flatter terrain and less of the physical type of protection offered by mountains.

During the Zhou dynasty, the compass was invented. This only helped to focus the attention to *direction* in developing a positive environment. Many practitioners of other philosophies like Taoism, contributed elements of their thinking to Feng Shui. Taoists used the compass in their study of the *I Ching*.

In the Han dynasty and after, Taoism was very popular with many wealthy Chinese and scholars. They began to use ideas found in Taoism and in the *I Ching* in many of their everyday practices. The different branches of Feng Shui

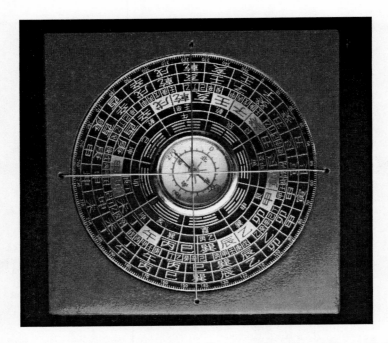

developed using these ingredients and the compass. The philosophy became much more complicated and technical, but the following thinking illustrates to what degree the Chinese believed Feng Shui affected a man's success in life:

> *The most important thing in man's success is his **Destiny**,*
> *Second is his **Luck**,*
> *Next comes his environment, or **Feng Shui**,*
> *A person's **Virtues** comes fourth,*
> *And finally comes **Education**.*

Some people who considered *Feng Shui* important to their welfare and success did not like the idea that things like their birth date—things that were "set in stone"—caused them to start at a disadvantage in their pursuit of their goals and aspirations. Users of *Feng Shui* were aware that there was nothing they could do to change the factors over which they had no control, such as destiny and luck. However, according to early believers, they could make corrections that would have a huge effect on their life's path . . . they could change their environment! A version of *Feng Shui*, known to many as **Compass**, was and still is the classical foundation for the philosophy. There are many branches of Compass Feng Shui that are still practiced today.

Feng Shui increasingly impacted the practices of Eastern cultures. The palaces and tombs of the royal family during the Tang dynasty (618 to 907) strictly followed the criteria of *Feng Shui*. When Buddhism reached into China, it absorbed the *Feng Shui* principles by combining them with their own practices. All of the historic Buddhist temples located in the mountains were constructed using *Feng Shui*. Many ancient sites like the Forbidden City in Beijing are laid out according to *Feng Shui* principles.

With the opening up of China to the West, *Feng Shui* became increasingly known and practiced by people outside China. The *Feng Shui* masters had and still have great influence with the buildings in Hong Kong. During British rule in Hong Kong, millions of dollars were paid in compensation to people who claimed their good *Feng Shui* was harmed by the building of government buildings and roads. These concepts are so embedded in the culture that newly opened *Disneyland Hong Kong* was carefully planned to include the elements of *Feng Shui* so important to the culture. Based on the recommendation of a *Feng Shui* master, the angles of the gates were altered 12 degrees, and a bend was placed in the walkway from the train station to the gate, so that the positive flow of energy will not be lost.

Although Feng Shui has been officially forbidden in the People's Republic of China since 1949, people still believe in the old ways. Or maybe they just want to be on the safe side. After all, why tempt fate?

Today, Feng Shui can be found all over the planet. If you ask someone from India if they use *Feng Shui*, they may have a blank look on their face. But, if you start to explain the philosophy, they will say, "*Oh, you mean Vastu!*". In Vietnam, Feng Shui is known as Phoy Thuy, while in Thailand, they know of this philosophy as Jewee. There are many different names for this environmental science that we in the West call Feng Shui.

The Practice of Feng Shui in the West

It is amazing how different populations developed their own ways of living a successful life by making changes to their environments. The most amazing thing is that they all have so many similarities!

Feng Shui gathered a big following in Europe before becoming an increasing factor in the United States. The British Isles are a true "hot bed" of use and development in this ancient philosophy. Many schools and consultants exist in the UK. In London, top soccer teams follow *Feng Shui* principles to insure their success.

Over the last 20 years, a new school has taken hold in different parts of the world, and especially in the United States. This new school has several names. One is Tibetan Black Hat. Like many followers I refer to it just as Black Hat.

DID YOU KNOW….
The earliest aim of Feng Shui was to maintain the harmony and balance between Heaven and Earth. The purpose of Feng Shui has always been to create environments in which Chi moves smoothly.

Even though this form of *Feng Shui* was brought over to the United States in 1986 by a Buddhist monk and Feng Shui master by the name of Thomas Lin Yun, it has a long and varied path of its own. Professor Lin Yun, who resides in San Francisco, still travels all over the world giving lectures and his thoughts on *Feng Shui*. He has been asked to speak at such different venues as Harvard and in Washington, DC. Black Hat *Feng Shui* is popular in the United States because it takes into account many western ideas, inventions, and life styles. For example, we take for granted our televisions, computers, microwaves, and electricity. This school of *Feng Shui* has "cures" or applications for them. This is the school in which I am trained, and that I use so successfully to get homes sold.

Black Hat *Feng Shui* is a wonderful combination of the strong traditions of the past . . . things that have always worked . . . and all of the latest findings about our present environment. A philosophy like this, built on flexibility and awareness of change, is effective for those very reasons . . . because it consistently reflects our rapidly changing environment and continues to add to it what is NEW!

Points to Remember

1. Early in man's development, location had to be considered strongly for survival.

2. The philosophy known as Feng Shui has made mistakes and many corrections along the way.
3. The cultivation of crops and the burial of ancestors where some of the earliest uses of Feng Shui.
4. I Ching is a major reference book for Feng Shui.
5. Earliest Feng Shui schools were Land Form and Compass. Black Hat is a school very popular in the United States.

Frequently Asked Questions

Is Feng Shui a religion?
No, it is not! It is a philosophy created through working with nature and common sense. This philosophy has been improved over many years by noticing what works and what doesn't.

Who can benefit from using this philosophy?
Anyone and everyone can use Feng Shui to improve their environment and their success. Many people around the world believe deeply in its power. Celebrities such as Donald Trump, Richard Branson, Oprah Winfrey, Madonna, and Catherine Zeta-Jones all consider *Feng Shui* before beginning a big project.

"The Tipi is much better to live in;
Always clean, warm in winter, cool in summer; easy to move.
The white man builds big house, cost much money,
like big cage, shut out sun, can never move; always sick."

Chief Flying Hawk
Oglala Sioux
1852-1931

CHAPTER 2

How Feng Shui is Changing the
Way We Sell Homes

Terry had been selling homes more than 25 years, but had never seen something so surprising. A home that had been on the market for well over a year had finally sold! He never thought someone would actually buy that wreck. He had shown the home twice without luck; its failure to sell didn't surprise him. It looked like the owners had been kidnapped back in the 70's, and everything had been left just waiting for their return!

The house had been listed, it seemed, with every agent in town, but he heard that the latest patsy had hired someone to do some crazy Chinese thing with the house. It was some word he couldn't pronounce. Crazy, that's all . . . it was crazy!!

Terry is not unique. Selling real estate has always been a process than is slow to change. The idea has been "if it works, don't break it"! There are agents who would rather the computer had never been created. After all, what was wrong with having the new listings being dropped off twice a week at the offices? They sometimes think that the world would be a better place, if the cell phone, the pager, websites, virtual tours, e-mail, etc. would just go away!

Many other fields consider staying the same a sure way of losing ground . . . . if you're not green and growing, then you must be ripe and rotting! To these folks, there are only two choices: you get better or you become obsolete. Dear old Terry may not like to hear it, but the real estate workplace is changing!

I entered the world of real estate sales twice, once in New Jersey in the late 70's and in the Carolinas in the early 90's, so I can tell you that things are indeed changing. Change is never easy on anyone, but for some folks it can be cause to consider working at Wal-Mart as a welcomer instead of (*gasp*) learning something new! Over the last five years, change has been coming fast and furious in the real estate industry. We have companies buying companies, and many independent real estate agents deciding to do business their own unique way. Their way may include charging a lower fee for their services or offering to just place a home in the Multiple Listing Service (MLS) for a flat fee . . . sometimes for as little as a few hundred dollars. The consumers—in our case, buyers and seller—are forcing our industry to evolve, even if we would rather it stayed "same old same old". Consumers are much better informed, and considerably more technology-saavy than they were fifteen or twenty years ago. We need to face this fact . . . or perish.

An agent today needs to really consider *how* things are changing in real estate. Years ago, we thought walk-in traffic would keep us in business. Today, the consumer has an ever-increasing range of choices, including conducting business over the Internet. While this may cause the "old-timers" to weep, we're never going to return to "the good old days". Realtors in some states, just recently, have tried very hard to enforce legislation that eliminates the so-called "discounter", but they have failed. The courts have ruled, and will continue to rule, that it only fair to let Mr. Flat Fee or Ms. Discount "play" the game. And by play, I mean have the opportunity to sell real estate their way and charge what they want. So, I think you better count on only one sure thing in the future . . . more change!

With the MLS information now being conveniently available to anyone who has Internet access and who wants to take a look, we need to understand that becoming unique in the field of real estate is more important than ever. We no longer have exclusive rights to the information about who has a home to sell, and exclusive control on what we'll charge to open up that front door to a potential buyer. We need to understand these ramifications and adjust.

Today's agents need to come up with a way to "set themselves apart" or they may be one of the many folks who get into our fine business and leave within a year or two without ever gaining a foothold. Or it can easily happen to you, Mr. or Ms. Veteran Agent. If you decide to stay in a world of where change doesn't happen, where technology is irrelevant, and new philosophies like Feng Shui are just "crazy", then you will end up like the poor dinosaur that could not adapt to a world of less food, less sunshine, and cooler temperatures.

Since you're reading this book, I'm figuring you are a real estate agent who not only wants to survive, but actually flourish in your career choice. You want to make sure that people see you as a problem-solver.

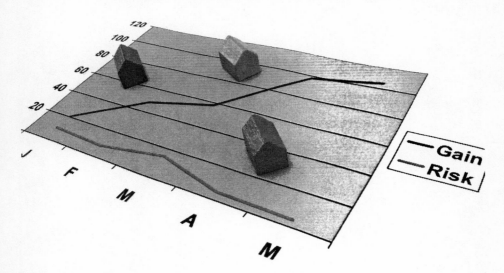

Your customers need to see that not only do you represent the solution to their problem, but you actually are able to offer a unique service to them . . . a service that represents an easier way to get a home sold. You need to decide

NOW to become something more than just a typical agent; you need to decide to become someone who offers something different.

I used the following little saying to attempt to set myself apart in the Charlotte, N.C. real estate market, and it worked for a while. I would tell a prospective listing that most agents use the "3 P's" marketing strategy: First they *PUT* your home into the MLS, then they *PLACE* a sign in the yard, and then they *PRAY* that another agent will bring you a qualified buyer. I tried to show them I did a little more than the average agent, and it did work. As I said earlier, an agent has to stand out to those folks who haven't decided who will list their home.

That is where Feng Shui comes in. Lets face it, some agents will continue to do just the 3 P's, and will make a living of sorts, and worse . . . will try to downplay the services agents who want to be creative and attentive offer to their clients. In my market, many real estate agents would be very negative about open houses, but I tried to use the Open House concept as a strategy to illustrate what I did, and did well! More importantly, I found that customers responded very powerfully to an agent who would and could help them prepare their home to show better than the house down the street.

This is one reason why Feng Shui appealed to me so much. I have used Feng Shui a great deal in my practice, and am constantly refining the process.

I first found the idea of moving some furniture to improve the flow to be very beneficial. Using accessories in rooms to add a particular color was immediately helpful. It's easy for anyone to understand why certain fragrances invoke a positive feeling in a buyer. These ideas just added up!

Where should I consider using Feng Shui?

You can break up the use of Feng Shui in a house into two categories . . . both of which are *TOTALLY* necessary to accomplish your mission. The first area that needs a lot of attention is the **OUTSIDE** of a home. We all know that curb appeal can solve many problems. Of course, the second area is the **INSIDE**. I always liked to put it this way to a client: "we *Feng Shui* the outside to attract buyers, and we *Feng Shui* the inside of a home to make it so comfortable that they don't ever want to leave". This philosophy has worked wonders for my homeowners over the years.

As an agent, you have heard about "Dressing a Home for Success", and it does work well. When we use *Feng Shui*, we take the same concepts even farther by incorporating the five senses, correcting imbalances inside and out, correcting (or curing) characteristics of a home that makes a potential buyer uneasy, and using color to create the feelings we want the visitor to have about the home.

Feng Shui is an environmental science. Modern day scientific research has begun to substantiate many of the concepts behind this ageless philosophy— ideas that promote those things that create enthusiasm and comfort for an individual. *Feng Shui* has been called by many "the Art of Placement" . . . and it is indeed that, but it is so much more! Fifteen years of home-selling experience, combined with "*Feng Shui* eyes" has given me a rare perspective on how to achieve a quick and successful sale of a home.

Exactly what does a Feng Shui agent do differently?

When I first pull up to a house that I'm working with, I notice many of the same things about its appearance that any agent might notice. But there's a major difference . . . I also am looking at *Feng Shui* problems. *Feng Shui* problems often affect people at a sub-conscious level; they may be totally unaware of the specific nature of the problem, but have a feeling of unease about the home right from the start.

As we get into each of the chapters, I will point out corrections or "cures"; in some cases, they will seem like common sense, and in others, they may not seem to totally make sense. However, these "cures" have been handed down over thousands of years. These solutions have been tried and tested, and create a more comforting and less worrisome environment for the owner and the visitor. The psychological sensitivity of humans to specific things is actually quite forceful, and being aware and making corrections around these things is very beneficial for the home seller. This acute sensitivity of human beings to their environment is what *Feng Shui* is all about. Although we have spent less time attending to these ideas in Western cultures, we are learning that if we can come closer to creating a "perfect" environment, many benefits are manifested.

Everyday, you try to get your homeowner to make changes that will affect how quickly a home sells, and for what price. These suggestions for change often include things like getting rid of clutter, mowing the yard, rearranging things to make a home's square footage look "bigger", getting rid of that bad aroma left by the dog, fixing the broken light fixture, or replacing the carpet.

With *Feng Shui*, we talk about all of these things too, but in a very different way. We will help you give your sellers psychological reasons why clutter is

---

DID YOU KNOW....
Many famous people and major companies use Feng Shui for their homes and businesses? To name a few: Donald Trump, Madonna, British Airways, Chase Manhattan Bank, Tommy Hilfiger, Coca Cola, CBS Studios, Bill Clinton, Oprah Winfrey, Panasonic, Steven Speilberg, and Kellogg's.

---

costing them a sale. We'll give you reasons why the color carpet they choose may get them (and you) more dollars, and you'll hear about how influencing the different senses make you (and more importantly the buyers) react differently.

Long ago I stopped taking a listing, no matter the price, if the seller wouldn't take some constructive criticism. To me, taking a listing and placing it on the market before the concerns are addressed is like committing suicide. It's stupid to place a home on the market when it is not in its best condition. The first several weeks are crucial! You are wasting your best time and opportunity to become a hero to the sellers by getting their home sold quickly for top dollar. Instead, you'll end up with a house that doesn't sell, and sellers who are motivated to make the changes you requested . . . . with the new agent they hired when they became upset with *you* for the market's slow response.

Feng Shui will give your listings that extra edge they need to stand out from the competition. *Feng Shui* will address all of the things that you sometimes feel self-conscious about bringing up to an owner . . . in a way that makes sense and gives them another reason to "get their act together". And let's face it, we need to get the owners working with us on a team. Without this "teamwork", it is so very difficult to accomplish the task at hand.

So, in the chapters that follow, we will explain step-by-step how to create powerful curb appeal that will make many more buyers to want to stop, pull a flyer, and call to have a look. Then we will go room by room giving you the criteria for a more pleasing environment so those buyers really won't want to leave! With this *Feng Shui* knowledge you will:

- *multiply your buyers and sellers;*
- *increase your referral base; and*
- *get rid of difficult listings!*

Points to Remember

The world of real estate is changing tremendously. You will need to change to survive. Never has it been more important for an agent to become "unique".

1. The first area that is given attention using Feng Shui in a home is the outside. You must improve the "curb appeal".
2. Feng Shui problems and their cures affect an individual on a subconscious level.
3. Never ever take a listing as-is. This will waste your time, energy, and finances.
4. Finally, if you help a buyer find a house with good *Feng Shui*, when the owner finally decide to sell and relists with you . . . you'll have a listing that is already much easier to sell!

Frequently Asked Questions

If being employed by the "biggest" real estate company is not the most important factor, what reasons should I stress to clients about hiring me as an agent?
Emphasize your ability to help them make their home show its absolute best. A home that covers all of the *Feng Shui* bases will sell much quicker and often for more money. A house that does not sell within the first 30 days often sticks around too long. Make the first five to ten showings a masterpiece, and often you can get the job done fast.

What is so important about dressing up the outside?
Curb appeal alone can increase "traffic" in the house dramatically. After all, it doesn't matter how nice it is on the inside if no one ever makes it that far! If your house is not inviting and attractive outside . . . add another month or two!

Isn't the inside more important?
Actually, no! The outside needs to be given priority with respect to selling a home.

Are buyers always aware of their feelings when looking at a home for the first time?
No. Their subconscious, or intuition, often sends off "red flags", and they don't exactly know why. They just know it doesn't "feel right". When people make these comments, pay specific attention to the areas where they seem to feel the most discomfort.

*"The mountains, rivers, earth, grasses, trees, and forests
are always emanating a subtle, precious light, day and night,
always emanating a subtle, precious sound,
demonstrating and expounding to all people
the unsurpassed ultimate truth"*

Yuan-Sou

CHAPTER 3

It's a Feeling . . . and it's all Energy!

Mary Lou and her husband Jack had been looking for a home with their agent for over three months. They had seen some nice homes in good locations, but nothing that felt "right". Their agent was becoming more and more frustrated. Any time a home in the north or west part of the city came on the market, she checked their criteria and called them immediately. But she was about to give up on working much longer with them. Even Mary Lou and Jack were beginning to wonder if they were being too picky.

*One day a home came on the market in one of the neighborhoods they liked, and an appointment was set for the next day. The minute Mary Lou and Jack walked into this home, they felt "different". They couldn't put a finger on it exactly . . . it just felt right. Somehow the entrance seemed especially positive, and there seemed to be so much more room . . . even though the MLS sheet said it was smaller than the last two homes they had turned down. The natural light coming in the house was wonderful and made them feel optimistic that they might **finally** have found their home.*

Although Mary Lou and Jack kept mentioning to each other how much they liked the house, they were almost afraid to show their agent too much pleasure. After three months of searching, they were sure that there had to be something wrong. But the moment they got into their car, their emotions bubbled over, and they called their agent within fifteen minutes to tell her . . . this is the one!

Earlier, I mentioned that the words Feng Shui stand for "wind" and "water". Keep this in mind as we cover this most important idea in Feng Shui. Wind and Water are the two main ways that energy is moved around our planet, and this happens every minute of every day. The primary focus of Feng Shui is to make sure that the energy that flows into your environment is positive and nourishing. Energy, or what the Chinese call *Chi*, is constantly in motion. Chi makes up everything . . . and I mean everything.

Energy moves . . . this is its nature. Our senses definitely are aware of more obvious forms of motion, but usually not such a subtle movement as that of energy. Its passage is invisible, but still a person can detect, at times, some uneasiness when sitting in certain areas of a room. These feelings can determine whether we want to linger or flee!

If you have any doubts to whether there are other realities or "feelings", animals and birds often live in a reality different from ours! Some can hear sounds that we can't. Some can see light frequencies that we can't. Many mammals (like dogs) live in a world of scents about which we have no knowledge. How about all those "waves" that move so easily around this world producing sound on a radio, pictures on a television, or voices on our cell phones? Sure, we can't see them, but if your idea of reality is what you can see . . . you are only considering a small fraction of what is really there. Hindu and Buddhist seers teach that the world of appearances is mere illusion, and there is something more powerful that is beneath the material world. It is this intangible world that is what is really important.

Albert Einstein's famous equation concludes that energy forms matter and when matter disperses it coverts back to energy. Every particle of existence is made of energy (Chi) and this energy explains all movement, changes and phenomena in our universe.

Many years ago, as microscopes improved, scientists began to find that when you break anything down to its smallest components, it is just energy . . . energy vibrating at different speeds. So . . . my desk is just energy? *Yes!* Is your new blouse just energy? Yes! How about my hamster? *Yes!* How about your youngest brother? *Yes* . . . he is, too . . . and he seems to have a lot of it!!

Quantum physics has made great strides in the examination of these tiniest of particles. These are not the atoms we all learned about in high school. No, these tiny particles are much, much smaller . . . and react very strangely. For one thing, the theory challenges the idea that properties of matter have an objective existence independent of observation. It seems that when these particles are observed, they exist in one form, but when our intention to observe them is not present . . . they no longer exist in that form. And if that is not strange enough, if a pair of these particles were present together at one time, and you split them up . . . an amazing thing happens when we do an experiment on one of the pair. The other reacts the same way, as if it were the one being worked on! And this happens if you place particle *A* on one side of the earth and Particle *B* on the other side! This notion of *entanglement* suggests that in the quantum world, objects are not independent if they have interacted with each other or come into being through the same process. They become linked, or entangled, such that changing one invariably affects the other, no matter how far apart they are—something Einstein called "spooky action at a distance".

DID YOU KNOW….
With the exploration of the subatomic world in the 20th century, the whole universe is now seen as endless motion and activity; in a continual cosmic dance of energy.

Intention, which has always been an important part of Feng Shui, seems to have found some measure of validity within the most sophisticated areas of scientific investigation. We all hope that our prayers or visualizations have a positive effect in our desired outcomes. More and more, it seems that we are acquiring scientific proof that this "spiritual" part of our lives is just as important to our physical well-being as our overt actions. There have been many studies around the notion that "putting something out there" in the universe is definitely a start to manifesting aspirations or dreams.

So, we know that making a change to the energy we encounter in our personal space has a great effect on outcomes in our personal lives. There are consequences if we move something or change something. *"Consequences"* is probably the wrong word . . . it is more like you have started a "chain reaction". Over the last twenty years, Quantum Physics has reinforced what Feng Shui users and Practitioners have known for thousands of years. They believe that everything is connected. We are not separate from our neighbor or our fellow employees . . . we have a connection . . . a connection that has always existed. We are connected to the animals and insects. We are connected in some way to everything that makes up our universe.

Many religions, especially Eastern religions, have long believed that on a quantum level, we are intertwined and if something happens to one of us, it takes a toll on all of us. Any decision that has an effect on our earth affects all of its creatures. This notion of energy, or Chi, is an important part of other philosophies like Tai Chi and Acupuncture, where it is thought to move through our bodies in channels called meridians.

The religious and philosophical texts of Taoists, Hindus, and Buddhists all conceive of the world in terms of movement, flow, and change. The Eastern mystics see the universe as an inseparable web, whose interconnections are very dynamic and not at all static. But surprisingly, so does modern physics!

So where am I heading with this? On a simple level, we want to exercise control of the energy that surrounds us. By simply moving an object, bringing in a live plant, changing the color of a room, or doing some weeding outside, the "feeling" of your environment will change. These actions actually produce that change! Following the advice of the Feng Shui experts can help create whatever environment you wish. If you want peace and tranquility, you can achieve it. If you want a place that permits you to reach your career goals, it can be done. If you desire to reinforce and improve relationships, this is possible. And if you want to make your home a powerful magnet for a potential homebuyer, this too can be achieved!

Often, when you show a home or enter a new environment, you somehow feel different. Now that "different" feeling can be anything from refreshing and welcoming to tiring and a little depressing. When selling a home, negative feelings are not what we are looking for. What we want is a mix of reactions that causes you to feel comfortable and enthusiastic about this space. Actually, if you don't feel these things in your present home, you need to make these corrections immediately. A home that is not providing you with feelings of empowerment is not helping you to become all that you can be! So you may want to forget other people's homes for the moment . . . and get moving on your own!

Once again, energy makes up everything, and Feng Shui can be seen as a manipulation of this dynamic source. Chi comes into our environments several ways, but the primary focus often is the front door of your home, apartment, or office. The front door is called *"The Mouth of Chi"*, and needs special attention no matter where you live, work, or play.

An environment is looked at as similar to a human body. Again, the front door is the mouth. The windows are the "eyes", and are also a major contributor of energy entering a space. The hallways and paths we take through an environment are our "veins", and move this life-force (Chi) through the "body" (our environment).

Just as with a person's body, there can be a blockage in a home. There can be a "health problem" with our environment. When we have a blockage in our veins, this can be very serious, and must be corrected . . . often with surgery. So, you may want to think of Feng Shui as a form of surgery for your home, office, or other living environments.

Does it make sense to make sure your front door easily opens? That it does not squeak or make an annoying sound when opened? Do you think keeping the entrance free of clutter would be important? Are sparkling windows important? Yes, all of these things are important, because we want to make sure that the energy that travels to and around the house is attracted into the home. Our environments need a new supply of Chi each and every day. Just like your body needs plenty of clean air to function at its best, our homes and offices do, too!

Well, you say *"What if I never use the front door? What if I prefer to enter my home through the garage?"* These are good questions. Even if you don't use it, the front door remains the "Mouth of Chi". So make sure you (or your homeowner) starts to use the front door more . . . at least once or twice a day, open it up! The "eyes" (windows) need to have special care also! It seems like the windows in our homes are often neglected and left to fend for themselves. Make cleaning the "eyes" a priority. Don't forget, we want lots of nourishing energy to enter our homes and offices.

There are several ways to be more appealing to this life source. The front of the house needs to be kept well groomed and attractive, and leaving lights on outside can help "lead" Chi to your front door. Make sure that mailbox is not run down and unattractive. We will get into "curb appeal" completely in an upcoming chapter, but for now just keep in mind: nice looking and well tended front doors attracts Chi!

The homes that are being built these days are very lovely and open, and most people seem to be looking for this type of home. But, from a Feng Shui point of view, there are problems in some of the home plans builders are now using. One BIG problem is that lots and lots of new homes have you entering the home and immediately seeing straight through the house to the backyard. Those soaring windows in the back of our homes are gorgeous, but Chi enters a home like this and quickly rushes through and back outside without taking its time to "meander" through a house, so that it nourishes the home. This energy needs to be checked. It needs to be manipulated.

We need to learn how to direct energy coming in to our environments. We need to create a detour. One way is to place a plant or plants in front of the flow, so it has to "go around" these objects. You can easily use other objects like statues or furniture. Often, you can place a plant in the direct path between the front door and the back windows. A water fountain is also a great "obstacle", and brings many other benefits to a home, which will be covered later. Remember, our goal is to redirect the "Chi", not to create a traffic flow problem by placing objects in the way of the people entering the front door.

Other Feng Shui cures, like hanging a crystal between the front door and the rear windows, are also very helpful. Understand that attracting and using this incoming energy correctly is VERY, VERY important to give your home a powerful, hidden boost in swaying a potential buyer to strongly consider your home.

Let's cover another way homes in the West lose this precious energy. DRAINS are a big problem, and we have them throughout the modern home and office. We might have more than one bathroom which has sinks, toilets, and a bath tub. We have a kitchen which has a sink. We probably have a utility room which has an outlet for water. All of these need special attention. The idea is the energy we took special precautions to entice may come in and quickly find the easiest way to escape, and that is going down a drain or toilet and leaving without giving our space any help.

So, get yourself and your homeowner in the habit of always closing the doors to all of the bathrooms and the utility room when not in use. Also, close all drains in the bathrooms, kitchen, and utility room when not using them. This will, at least, insure that our Chi will stay longer and have a much better chance of making our house or office feel good, safe, and comfortable.

Energy or Chi is important to making your home feel like a home. Keep these ideas in mind when trying to sell a home, or just when trying to improve the quality of your environment . . . it's worth making them a habit!

Points To Remember

1) Energy, known as Chi, is always in motion.
2) Everything is connected. A change of any sort has a reaction.
3) Intention does produce an effect.
4) We can produce the feelings in a home that are necessary to sell it. Those feelings include comfort and enthusiasm.
5) The front door is the major power source for energy entering our home, and is referred to as "*The Mouth of Chi*".
6) We need to stop allowing Chi to enter our home, and be allowed to leave quickly. Close doors to a utility room and all bathrooms. Keep toilet seats always down, when not in use.
7) A plant, statue, or fountain can be used as an obstacle to make energy move around it and stop it from rushing through.

Frequently Asked Questions

How do you pronounce Chi?
It is pronounced "Chee". And you can see it spelled *Chi* or *Qi.*

Is Chi just in living things?
No . . . it is in everything . . . walls, chairs, clouds, clothing, etc.

What if we never use our front door?
It still remains the "Mouth of Chi". Try to open it once in a while.

If you notice my scowl and mutter
It is because of this infernal clutter

There is an excessive pile of papers and letters
Here is one of messages, it does not get better.

There is so much exasperation
Matched only by my frustration

Excerpted from *Clutter*
by Irving Kaufman

CHAPTER 4

Flow and Clutter

The Morans had placed their large two-story home on and off the market with three different agents over a ten-month period. By this point, they were beginning to believe that all agents were worthless, and that the value of their home was not appreciated by either the agents or their clients. The Morans were considering placing their home on the market "For Sale By Owner". They figured they couldn't be any less effective than the real estate agents.

They decided to talk with one more agent, who had been referred to them by a mutual friend. According to the friend, this agent was different and used something called "Feng Shui" to get homes sold. Although they had heard of Feng Shui, they couldn't see how it would make much difference. However, out of friendship they decided to at least meet with this new guy.

*When Randy arrived, he went on and on about things they had never heard of, but some things sort of made sense. One idea especially sounded good. Their last two agents kept giving them feedback from potential buyers about how **small** their home felt. They had pretty much discounted this feedback because their home was bigger than the house across the street . . . a house that sold in less than three weeks, and for more money than the Morans were asking for their own home. And to top it off, their lot was much nicer!*

But Randy's emphasis on getting rid of the clutter in their home started to make sense. He had mentioned that clutter was in many places in a home, some that most folks never thought of . . . and kept emphasizing *that "decluttering" not only made the house feel bigger . . . it improved something called **Chi**.*

The Morans decided to give Randy a try and hired him that night. They followed Randy's directions on how to get rid of clutter throughout their house, then they added a few recommended touches in some of the rooms, and waited. Well . . . it didn't take long. On the very first showing, the potential buyer remarked on the great flow to the house, and even came back a second time . . . how exciting! The next weekend, things exploded as four showings were scheduled; suddenly, the Morans had two couples fighting over their previously "unsellable" home. The final offer ended up getting them $2,000 more than what they expected, and they finally were able to move out of the city.

Feng Shui is often called *The Art of Placement*. When we place things in such a way that it interferes with our ability to move comfortably, this is certainly a poor flow for our Chi. The impact of this situation is multiplied when a home is for sale. First, the home feels smaller than it really is. Secondly, this placement gives our visitors . . . we'll call them Mr. or Ms. Buyer . . . an uneasy feeling about the home. They wonder, *"Will I have room for my furniture? What if I bump into something while I'm here?"* They begin to ask, *"Does it feel too close in here? Can this house ever feel like my "home sweet home"? Is this really a good floor plan for me?* Then they begin to question, *"Is all this clutter hiding something? Is this home well-maintained? Will I be spending a lot of my time fixing things?"*

Don't ever give a buyer a chance to question whether your home can be a good fit! Once a buyer starts to ask these questions, the sale is probably lost. Think of the buyers as carrying two mental folders. One folder holds each positive feeling that they get from your home, and the other holds anything negative that comes up during the visit. The trick is to always be in command of that positive folder throughout a showing.

Don't let the potential buyers fill up the negative folder and start to dwell on these things. You want them to come in the front door, immediately see the first great feature of your home and add a mental reaction or comment to the positive folder. We want to be able to orchestrate the showings as much as possible to generate those positive feelings.

When most people enter an uncluttered space, the natural tendency is to turn right. If your living room is on the right when the buyers enter, make sure you impress them with the size and features of this space. If you have a fireplace in this room, highlight it BIG time by bringing it to their attention immediately. Ways to highlight a fireplace include the use of lights, a beautiful painting sitting on the mantle, or some bright flowers on the hearth. If the fireplace is the primary feature of this room . . . make it STAND OUT! Orchestrate the "flow" of the showing by highlighting the best things in each room in a way that draws the viewer to these items or features.

So, flow and lack of clutter are of utmost importance in Feng Shui. If your home is cluttered, all bets are off where the potential buyers will head when they come in the door. Before they even come through the door, you have already lost the ability to influence what they see and how they react!

Make the visit totally pleasant for the buyer by getting rid of excessive furniture, books, and "collectibles". No matter how much you love your "collection", you want the buyer's conscious attention focused on square footage . . . a good thing! But on the subconscious level, they will also "feel" comfortable, unrushed, and curious. They will be asking *"What special feature will we see next? I bet the rest of the house is just as comfortable! I can't wait to see the other rooms."* The bottom line in Feng Shui is . . . . NO CLUTTER!

Many books and several Feng Shui trainers say that if you only take one thing from this whole philosophy and apply it . . . get rid of clutter! Getting rid of clutter will have serious positive consequences for anyone attempting to improve overall quality of life. And if you are selling your home, getting rid of clutter will quicken your sale and add dollars in your pocket!

There are many places that we hide things, collect things, and forget things. In this chapter, we'll explore a few. By clearing up clutter of all types, we change the feeling or the atmosphere. It's this "feeling" that we are after. Don't think that cluttered drawers or stacks of boxes in the back closet don't matter! You know they are there . . . waiting for you. Even though the simple idea of deleting old word processing files may seem like we are going a bit too far, it helps clear out the feelings that are prevalent when our lives are scattered and disorganized. Feng Shui is about changing feelings! You want a feeling of comfort, peace, and order.

Helpful-hint sources recommend all sorts of storage solutions such as shelves above doors, hooks on the backs of doors, peg-board for tools and small appliances, and under the bed storage. Storage organizers are masters at using every inch of a closet with shelf dividers, multiple hanging rods, and see-through bins and containers. What they don't realize is that, from a feng shui perspective, these techniques can cause as many problems as they solve. While well-organized clutter is certainly better than disorganized clutter, it's still there, interfering with the sense of openness and space. And from a buyer's perspective, it still raises the question, *"Where will I put my stuff?"*.

DID YOU KNOW...
Clearing clutter can actually release huge amounts of energy in your body. When you rid things in your life that no longer have meaning, you literally feel lighter!

Let's start with a living room or den. Typically, houses have too much furniture, too many family items, piles of books, accumulated newspapers, knick-knacks, toys, and . . . . artwork. Yes, your walls can also be cluttered! When selling your home, reduce picture overload, especially family photos. Reaction to art is very personal. If you have too many pictures on the wall, the buyer can lose concentration. If you have too many personal photos, the buyers place you in the home as the owner, and then can't see themselves as potential occupants. Either way . . . you lose! Don't allow the potential buyer to be more curious about the owner than about the house itself.

When I enter a home, excessive furniture is almost always present. Humans seem to be genetically pre-programmed to never throw anything out! Remember our friends, Clarence and Jill, living back in the cave days? Stocking up was a smart thing to do when the bison might not turn up in the neighborhood for a while, and surviving a cold winter depended on how much firewood you had stored in the back of the cave. It made sense to save things because these items were necessities. Today, we carry things a little too far. We rarely buy just what we need and we save more than we'll ever use.

Often, a living room or den will have at least one too many chairs and an extra table and lamp. If there is a book case, it often overflows with books, and there is seldom an empty space. For bookcases, start reducing clutter by eliminating 25% of the books, and then arrange the books by size and color, placing the larger and darker books on the bottom shelves. Then art can be added to create pockets of color and interest.

When energy comes into rooms that are disorganized and full of "stuff", the energy either can't get through easily or becomes stagnant and stops being of any help. If the energy doesn't have a way of moving through the floor plan . . . in other words . . . it doesn't "flow", the rooms adjacent to this room also do not get nourished properly, and have less energy. When energy stagnates, it ruins the energy in the room and begins to kill the potential sale of a home in many ways.

So, begin by reducing the furniture that blocks movement of both people and energy. And then check out the remaining furniture for clutter, especially side tables and their drawers. Clean these drawers out, as they keep you from totally achieving the feeling that you are after; you might also be surprised at how often a potential buyer opens drawers and closets to see if your clutter-free environment is "for real". Nothing destroys the potential buyers' trust faster than discovering everything has been shoved under the bed just before the showing. You want to positively affect your lifestyle by creating a habit for the "clutter-less" environment, and you want the buyer to know it's for real!

Speaking of clutter, the eating areas, both breakfast areas and dining rooms often end up with all sorts of things on the tables . . . . things that are unrelated to eating! Keep tables totally clear of irrelevant items. The only thing you should place on the table is a nice centerpiece that will attract the buyer's eye as he or she does a visual sweep when entering the room. If your table has sharp corners, place a table cloth over the table to cut down on aggravating edges. If the table is really beautiful, and you would rather not cover it, monitor its effect. Ask you agent to give you feedback on the potential buyer's reaction, or get an "honest" reaction to your room from a friend who will actually tell you the truth. You may have to make changes! Just as with the den and living room, if you have hutches or furniture with drawers in them . . . clean them out . . . you are moving anyway, so get a head start on the packing! Remember, it's a feeling, and whether the clutter is hidden or obvious, it has a negative affect at a subconscious level.

The kitchen is always a BIG culprit in the clutter war. Obvious clutter, which **must** be removed, is on the counter tops. Leave nothing on the counter tops other than a nice plant for the buyers' eyes to admire.

If you have a microwave or toaster on the counter that you use a lot . . . I'm sorry . . . put it into an accessible part of your cabinets or in the pantry. It's still there for you to use when needed, but your potential buyer doesn't need to see it. This is not a time to compromise. Your counter space, or lack of it, will have a huge impact on the selling of your home. If you're not sure what should be put away, try visiting a model home . . . . you will never see a toaster or mixer out on a counter. They understand what they are selling.

In our society, the refrigerator has become a walking billboard for information . . . your favorite take-out menu, magnetic calendars from irritating real estate agents, the dog's grooming appointment, and your children's artwork. It **must** be totally cleared off . . . . that's right . . . even little Millie's self-portrait! The top of a refrigerator is also a great place for stagnant Chi to collect. Often, this area hasn't been cleaned for years . . . and this is an outstanding time to do it.

As stated earlier, a potential buyer will look in some odd places when visiting your home. The sink must never have dirty dishes. The cabinets must be decluttered and reorganized. A good way to organize canned goods is to line them up from biggest to smallest with the labels all pointing the same way. Don't forget the tops of your cabinets . . . some people place way too much stuff on top of their cabinets, even though it is ornamental. This can add to a buyer's final judgment of *"no room for my stuff in this house"*.

The pantry has become very important for discriminating buyers. Just like you, they're looking for space for all of their things. So, reduce your pantry contents as much as 40% to 50% and organize it like your canned goods. Don't fail on this one . . . make it show big!!

One last thing about the kitchen; often the male buyers love to look under the sink. Once again, organize and reduce unnecessary items and make sure there is NO indication of a leak! All of these places have to be looking their best!

Let me once more review the reasons why things must look great. On a conscious level, less clutter throughout your house will create the feeling of a larger and well-maintained space. On a sub-conscious level, less clutter creates a feeling that is overpoweringly positive for you, and anyone visiting your home . . . . the feeling that your life is under control. Both are tremendously important to achieve your goal.

While we are reducing clutter and introducing control, let's not forget the bathrooms. The bathrooms need to be addressed in the same manner as the kitchen. Make sure the tub and the sink are clean and spotless, and that you have no items on the countertop. One plant would be nice, but no more. Declutter those cabinets and put away the toothbrush and Waterpik . . . nothing turns a buyer off any faster than the sight of your personal hygiene items. Be sure to watch out for the throw rug syndrome here. Multiple rugs often cover up bathroom floors, and create a feeling of smallness. Sometimes they are of different or incompatible colors. They distract from the buyer's perception of square footage in your bathroom, and may suggest you're hiding something.

Hallways can also give off a clutter alarm. Too many family photos or pictures can give a closed-in feel. Again, we do not want our buyers focusing on your lives and forgetting their actual assignment . . . to find a home and visualize themselves living there. If the hallway is dark, removing some of the artwork, and placing a mirror at one end will reflect light and will help move the Chi.

Too often, people forget about decluttering their garages and utility rooms. Don't expect a buyer to remember these rooms as positive features without a little help from you. Many sellers believe buyers will just look around the mess . . . after all, it will leave with you when you move out! But studies have shown this doesn't happen. It never happens. The buyer just remembers a small cramped space with too little room for their needs. So make every room and every space a positive experience for the potential buyer.

The outside of your home is another important part of the clutter saga. Please don't expect people to not "see" things. If your driveway is full of parked cars, trailers, or boats, they can't picture getting their cars in this cramped space. If you have a cluttered weedy flowerbed, work to make it a positive feature. Again, don't expect the buyer to be able to visualize it looking good. They can't, and they won't!

So ensure the yard looks well maintained and organized; otherwise, this adds to the buyers' feelings of clutter . . . that dreaded "four letter" word in Feng Shui.

Points to Remember

1) Clutter affects everyone on two levels . . . conscious perception and an unconscious sense that life is disorganized and out of control.
2) Clutter is the single most important item to correct in Feng Shui.
3) Clutter is everywhere . . . inside and outside.
4) Clutter is not always obvious; it can hide and impact the environment and a person's mental attitude.

Frequently Asked Questions

Why is Feng Shui often referred to as the Art of Placement?
Because placing things in a particular spot can have an adverse effect, while placing them somewhere else can have a positive impact.

Won't people always come up with something that is wrong with a house?
Probably yes, but we need to make sure they have to work to find the very few objections, while the many positives are obvious. The more "problems" they see, or imagine, the less consideration they will give your home. We want to give them little ammunition to say NO!

Why do you say people usually turn right when entering an environment?
Because most people are right handed. Think about when you drive . . . most people feel more comfortable making a right turn. Left turns are less safe! So using this fact can allow us to orchestrate a showing better.

You talk about highlighting a feature in a room. What if there is nothing to highlight?

This is only possible if you make it possible! Even in a vacant room, we can highlight the window or windows by placing a floor plant next to it. If a room has no windows, highlight its purpose. A bedroom can be highlighted by turning on the side table lights, and clearing everything else out of the room. If your kitchen is somewhat "blah", place a lovely vibrant plant on the counter under your cabinets or put down a single colorful floor rug to attract the buyers' line of vision when they walk in and notice the lovely floors. No matter what room, create a focal point for the potential buyers when they walk in.

You say they will look in drawers and closets and under sinks. Will this really have an effect?

Yes . . . it all does! You are building their trust in how you maintain a home. You are leading them to believe that this home is a "cinch" to live in.

What is wrong with placing things on top of the cabinets in the kitchen or in a bathroom?

Nothing, but we usually don't stop with a couple of items. We become accustomed to these items and just don't see them any more, but for visitors, these areas conjure up a feeling of "too much".

Who has seen the wind?
Neither I nor you.
But when the leaves hang trembling,
The wind is passing through.

Who has seen the wind?
Neither you nor I.
But when the trees bow down their heads,
The wind is passing by.

Christina Georgina Rossetti
(1830-1894)

CHAPTER 5

The Yin and Yang Perspective

Donna was having some trouble getting to sleep in her new home, but that was nothing compared to her daughter, Brittany. Almost every night, Brittany was leaving her room and heading for her mom's bedroom. Donna had never had a problem with Brittany at their old home, so she wasn't really sure what was creating this new situation, which was contributing to her own sleep deprivation problem.

Brittany couldn't explain it. She just didn't feel comfortable after spending more than a few hours in her own bedroom. Donna had tried banning television after 7 PM, giving her hot milk before bed, and even reading stories to her . . . but nothing seemed to work.

This went on for a couple of months, affecting Donna's work and Brittany's success in 2nd grade. Finally, a friend suggested changing Brittany's room and encouraged Donna to talk with a Feng Shui expert about the energy in Brittany's room. The consultant didn't need much time to notice several glaring problems that could easily disrupt a person's sleep pattern. The bed was not in a secure position . . . so the bed was moved. But another change was just as important. The room was overly Yang, and needed to be toned down and made more Yin. Just changing the wall color was a huge success, allowing Brittany to finally feel less active at night and get uninterrupted rest.

One of the earliest measuring sticks for determining a property's imbalances was the use of "light" and "shade". Some environments had too much of one or too little of another. The Tai Chi symbol or the Yin-Yang symbol is famous throughout the world. Just as it originally represented light and shade, it has come to be used by the Chinese and other Feng Shui users to represent many things.

Words that define a Yang feeling or environment are words like active, aggressive, day, exterior, outside, male, summer, and light. On the Yin side, we find words like passive, retired, night, interior, inside, female, winter, and dark.

Here are some more examples of Yin and Yang words:

YIN	YANG
Moon	Sun
Low	High
Stillness	Movement
Odd Numbers	Even Numbers
Earth	Heaven
Cold	Hot
Soft	Hard
Valleys	Hills
Feminine	Masculine
Sleep	Wakefulness
Downward	Upward
Water	Fire
Mother	Father
Daughter	Son
Back	Front
Sour	Sweet
Sad	Angry
Rain	Sunshine
Small	Large
Dull	Sharp
Curved	Straight
Floral	Plaid

Try not to just think of these ideas as opposites, but more as complements. They are both sides of the same coin . . . you can't have one without the other. After all, you can't really define something without its (so-called) opposite.

Here is another list of Yin and Yang words for building sites:

YIN	_YANG_
Valley	Mountain Top
Small Town	Large City
Quiet Street	Busy Road
Forest	Desert
Shady Side of Street	Sunny Side
Single Level	High Rise Condo
Small Home	Large Home

Another intriguing thing to keep in mind when working with these pairs is that you can NEVER have a totally Yang environment or a totally Yin one . . . it is not possible and you wouldn't want one anyway! Every situation and every person has at least a little Yin or Yang. For that reason, _balance_ is a KEY idea when working with Feng Shui, but your definition of balance and that of a Feng Shui Consultant might be very different.

While we tend to think of "balance" as an equal or even mix, a 50/50 proposition or mix is not "good balance" in Feng Shui. Each area or room has different qualities and functions. One room might be perfectly balanced if it was dark and serene with just a hint of light . . . and another would be totally correct if it had tons of light and just a smattering of some dark blue or black mixed in. It depends on many factors but the appropriate proportion of Yin and Yang has much to do with room purpose.

It should be no surprise that a bedroom should be mostly Yin, while a room like the kitchen or a den needs to be more Yang. When possible, an important rule to follow is to have your Yang rooms towards the front of a house where most of the entertainment and interaction occurs, and the Yin rooms in the back for rest and quiet.

Consideration of the purpose of an area is especially important at the entrance. When you walk into a house from the front door, you do NOT want the area to be uninviting, dark, and non-welcoming. If you are attempting to sell a house, you especially do NOT want this kind of beginning for your showing. A foyer needs to say *"Welcome home"*. It needs to generate a feeling of *"Its great to be home, and I'm so fortunate I live here!"*. Overly Yin foyers can be dull, and could help the potential buyers make up their minds to reject your home immediately. Once that happens, it is really tough to get them back in a mode of considering your home as a possible purchase. You may have heard that a buyer will make up his or her mind within the first 15 to 30 seconds whether to consider a home for purchase . . . you don't want those critical 15 to 30 seconds lost!

Well, guess what . . . we can lose them outside with poor curb appeal, or lose them at the entrance, or in the foyer, or in the living room, or in the kitchen, and so on. Or we can take control from the start, and make sure that each step is a reward, and a reason to anticipate the next wonderful part of this house.

One way to create this anticipation is to take care to ensure the perfect balance of Yin and Yang for each room. The foyer needs to have more zip . . . more Yang . . . to it. Make sure the foyer is well lit and that lights are on during all showings. A mirror hanging on a side wall, *not* facing the front door, would create spaciousness and add more light. The color of the walls should be slightly Yang; colors like pale yellow, light beige, or a sage green would work well. You want this area to convey a sense of welcome. Make sure it is light . . . not dark, is not over populated with personal items, and radiates warmth.

In our society, a living room is often more a more formal area than a den, and often is located at the front of a home. While this area is probably not used as much as the more comfortable den, it should have a good mixture of Yin and Yang. Again, purpose should be considered. A room like this may often be used by a member of the family to read or get away for quiet contemplation. If this is the case, use of Yin colors may be more in line than something bright that caters to a social gathering. However, since our formal rooms are often used for entertaining, the mix in this particular room should usually be more Yang, with a good measure of Yin. One way to achieve this mix is to make sure the wall color is somewhat like the foyer . . . such as pale yellow. The floors need special attention, and once again, go for a Yang feeling . . . just don't overdo it. If the floor is all wood, go with a circular carpet in the middle of the floor that softens the edges of the room and pulls the eye to the center. Choose a carpet with some bright colors, such as red or yellow, and some subdued colors such as blue, black, and dark green. Don't go crazy in here!!

Since we want your potential buyer to start off moving through your space easily with no blockage, this first room needs to be more bare than full. Don't forget, most people will enter and turn right . . . so make the first room they encounter REALLY spacious and well-lighted. We need to fuel their excitement . . . not douse it immediately. This area of the house will also correspond to a particular part of an energy map that we will explore in Chapter Seven. As we progress through the book, we will review this tool very carefully for all areas of a house, but for now, just understand that this energy map will give us a lot more information to use when we are choosing color and accessories for an area.

If this room is not the living room but is instead the dining room, we must once again consider purpose. Do not use Yang colors for the walls! Although red has become a very popular color for dining rooms, it is an aggressive Yang color that encourages rapid eating. Fast food restaurants choose it for a reason! Instead, select a mid-range Yin color, such as sage green, a medium blue, or an earth tone, but do not use anything too dark like Forest Green. This would be too Yin and will relax your guests too much. While we don't want our guests wolfing down their food in a red dining room, we don't want them falling asleep over dessert! Bring in the Yang features with accessories such as red place mats, yellow flower arrangements, or colorful candles.

The kitchen is one of the most important rooms in your house with respect to Feng Shui. FIRST, make sure this area is sparkling clean. In Feng Shui thinking, the kitchen is where the preparer puts energy into the nourishment that will be taken in by the rest of the family. If this area is not organized and extremely clean, then it is out of balance, and everyone who resides here will be affected adversely with respect to their health, their attitude towards life and their goals, and their production at work. If you're selling the home, a kitchen needs to WOW the potential buyers, even if they never plan to cook at all! It may be surprising, but buyers who eat out every day will still be adamant about the kitchen being something special. A kitchen in our society seems to be a gathering place. It needs to look good!

With respect to the Yin/Yang breakdown, a kitchen is no way a Yin area. The kitchen and everything that goes on in here is decisively Yang. While many followers of Feng Shui think a kitchen represents purity and should be mostly white, this will probably not match the tastes of most buyers. Yellow, orange, earth tones, and beige would be good colors to pick. Just remember that this area tends to have a lot going on, and needs to keep focus and stay uncluttered. Do not use much, if any, of the color red in here.

DID YOU KNOW...

Turning on the spot lighting under the cabinets, and turning off the overhead light in a kitchen makes it more *Yin*. In a living room that has a glass coffee table, you can cover the table up with fabric to decrease the Yang aspect.

Each room in your house will lean toward one side of the Yin/Yang spectrum. In other words, more Yin is appropriate one place, while more Yang is appropriate in another. For example, bedrooms need to be more Yin, but too often they are not! This not only disturbs the individual's sleep, but can also hurt the prospective buyers' ability to see this room as a comfortable bedroom where they want to relax!

If buyers look at a room and have to guess its purpose, you have a BIG problem. Don't forget, you want to lead them through the house showing off its many great features, not playing "three guesses". It would make sense that if I use one of my bedrooms as an office, it can still become a bedroom again. Or if I use the dining room for a children's play area, the buyers surely understand it can be turned back into a dining room. Wrong! While the buyers may know this on a rational level, their emotions may be putting a negative comment into that mental folder we discussed earlier.

You must show each room off for what it was intended. If it is a dining room, the buyers expect some type of dining set up. Otherwise, you confuse them and allow them to leave thinking your home doesn't totally take care of their needs, even though it probably does. They probably have already seen five or more other homes, and if your dining room doesn't look like a dining room . . . guess what . . . they will remember your home as lacking a dining room! Or maybe you are using a bedroom for your office. They will remember later that they needed three bedrooms, and yours didn't add up. Don't expect them to figure things out!

So, if a room was a bedroom, make it a bedroom and make it more Yin. If this means painting it a more restful color and bringing in a old poster bed . . . do it. Stage it! Although it may inconvenience you for the moment, it will pay off. Rooms that should be mostly Yin are bedrooms and bathrooms. Rooms that need to be mostly Yang are kitchens, dens, recreation rooms, and breakfast areas. Rooms to make slightly more Yang than Yin are living rooms, foyers, and offices.

Have fun with Yin and Yang. Monitor your feelings and activities when using each room. If the room is an area you favor for reading, and you can't fully concentrate because it seems to be too Yang, . . . change it! But, please remember the goal of this book. We are not attempting to make this home perfect so you can keep living here. We want to satisfy the majority of potential home buyers who will be considering your home along with many others. We must not confuse them. We must use Yin/Yang successfully to convince them that that every room has a specific purpose that matches their every need.

Points to Remember:

1) Yin and Yang are complements, and not really opposites
2) When attempting to sell, each room needs to be obvious in its use
3) Don't allow the buyer to guess what a room was designed for . . . make it obvious!
4) Bedrooms need to be primarily Yin
5) The kitchen and den need to be mostly Yang

Frequently Asked Questions

In the Yin/Yang symbol (Tai Chi) there are always little dots of the opposite shade. What does this represent?
This means that no matter how Yin or Yang a person, place, or thing may be . . . that it still has to have some of its complement. Nothing is all Yin or all Yang.

If the house is built on a Yin site, do we have to take this into consideration for the house?
Yes you do! If the house is to be built in a valley, make sure the house is slightly more Yang by use of color and hopefully the amount of sun light. A red door or an exterior color like yellow will help bring a balance to this home.

Should all bedrooms be Yin?
Yes, most definitely! Especially when trying to sell a house, don't confuse an easily confused buyer by making a bedroom or bedrooms Yang. If you are living in the home, it is in your best interest to make sure you get a good night's sleep. An overly Yang bedroom can greatly interfere with how restful your sleep is.

I really prefer dark colors even for my front foyer. Is this problem?
It is if you are trying to sell a home! A dark, Yin foyer is a real turn-off for a visitor. Don't make the mistake of making them dislike your home immediately. If your home has a dark foyer, change it! After all, you're planning to move . . . save that favorite color for your new place.

What colors are Yin and what do you consider Yang?
All shades of red, yellow, and orange are definitely Yang. Purple, blue, and green are Yin. However, you can take any color that is dark and brighten is up by adding white or grey to it. This will definitely make it more Yang. Of course the same thing works with Yang colors—just add black and brown to it to make it more Yin.

What rooms have to show as Yang?
The kitchen MUST show as Yang, but dens and any room used for social gathering should be more Yang than Yin.

The flame crackles,
Splitting shinning sparks
And ashes and fire
Into the warming air.

It's always fighting
It's always changing,
Seems always so close
To life.

Excerpted from *Fire*
By Sandra Osborne

CHAPTER 6

The Five Elements

Darryl worked out of his home office most of the time, and wanted to make sure everything in his life was set up to help propel him towards achieving his financial goals. He had experienced great success since he started his home-based business in his previous home, but since moving to his current home, things had flattened out.

He loved his new home. He was especially proud that he was able to purchase it after doubling his business each of the last three years, but now something didn't feel quite right. Business was off 40 to 50% since moving into his new home office.

After several months in the new place, Darryl's wife, Karen, went to a Feng Shui workshop, and had been impressed with the ideas of making the energy in a space more nourishing and more powerful. She had re-arranged some of the furniture and belongings in her office downtown, to her great satisfaction. She had been remarking to Darryl for days about feeling more energetic and getting more done in less time.

When Darryl brought up his concern for his own business, Karen was quite enthusiastic about giving Feng Shui a chance in Darryl's office and possibly throughout their new home. She checked Darryl's office against the information she had acquired in the workshop, and noted it lacked two of the Five Elements she had studied. This imbalance began to correct itself slowly after she added just a touch of Fire and a touch of Metal to his office. After a week, some positive changes took place, but she decided to add just a little more Fire . . . and things started to get really interesting. Darryl was suddenly feeling like his old self and the phone started ringing consistently.

The Chinese have brilliantly used five natural elements prevalent in the world to represent five different types of energy in an environment. Our environments can be inside or outside. We can be discussing a home, an office, or an apartment. These Five Elements are tremendously important when making sure a home shows its very best. Most homes in the United States do not do a good job of taking into account these elements and their different traits and therefore their strengths.

The Five Elements are **WOOD, WATER, FIRE, EARTH** and **METAL.**

Each element is associated with specific colors, symbols, and shapes that represent this specific type of energy in an area. In the United States, homes tend to have an abundance of Wood and Earth, and often are deficient in the other elements. As with our discussion of the Yin/Yang balance, this needs to be rectified, so that each room has the correct balance. Once again, your definition of balance and a Feng Shui Consultant's definition would probably be quite different. As with Yin and Yang, a perfect split never works. Each room or environment has dominating elements. We do NOT want each element represented 20% of the time, but we do want some of each element all the time. We can accomplish this in a variety of ways, through the use of the colors, symbols and shapes that represent each element.

The Five Elements

	Water	Blue Black	Water Features & Fountains Mirrors	
	Wood	Green	Wood floors Furniture	
	Fire	Red	Candles Fireplace	
	Earth	Yellow Orange Brown	Ceramic Tile Clay pots	
	Metal	White Gray Silver Gold	Lamps Metal Objects Balls	

When someone walks into a room for the first time, a negative perception of the area may be caused by the lack of one or two elements. Perhaps there is an overabundance of one element to the exclusion of others. While we need to have each element present, often we only need small doses. When you find the need to bring in a missing element or two, you should begin considering different accessories to create this balance.

For example, when I mention to a client that they need to bring some Fire into their living room, I am NOT expecting them to paint the room red. But I do want them to bring in a red pillow or two, a set of red pillar candles, or possibly a pyramid or triangle. Small changes often do the trick; we have to monitor our reaction to these small changes first, and then act more strongly if necessary. This is a very important thing to remember . . . start with less and go to more.

As I stated earlier, many homes in our society have too much Wood and Earth. Our homes often have hardwood floors, wooden furniture, wooden frames around the artwork, green walls, and pictures on the walls showing forests or meadows. Because wood is a cultural expectation in our society, the owners probably don't think they are out of balance. With respect to Earth, we have tile floors, granite countertops, earthen pots, stone fireplaces, pictures on the walls showing mountains, and earth tones on all the walls. Sound familiar?

Real estate agents have been telling homeowners over and over to keep their homes "neutral". As a result, our homes are often void of any color, excitement or originality. Now I'm not leading a revolt on the "neutral" motto, but we have gone too far! Start considering ways to add some color to each room. You don't want to go crazy, but you might begin by picking up some pillows, candles, artwork, or area rugs to help balance the elements throughout your house.

Often people jump to the conclusion that painting is the answer. Paint is often a cheap and powerful way to freshen up a room. It has the added benefit of eliminating any unwanted odors from the dog or cigarette smoke. Painting a room is sometimes a GREAT idea, but again . . . be careful. Too much of certain colors may erase the good things a room already has. If you are considering painting, try one accent wall first and live a few days with it. Does it feel good? Does it make you feel better . . . more positive? Does it enhance other aspects of a room; for example, does it highlight the wood trim?

Please be especially careful with aggressive Yang colors like orange, yellow, and red. These colors may be too powerful for the potential buyer to even consider, immediately putting a negative comment in that mental folder we discussed earlier. Don't kid yourself; potential buyers will pick apart everything in your house in order to talk themselves out of making the "BIG" decision. Psychologists called it *cognitive dissonance* . . . the closer you get to a big decision, the more weight you give to the "negative" aspects of the decision. If your furniture is pretty sorry, they'll talk about it. If your paint colors are too vibrant, they'll talk about it. If your cleaning habits are not the best, they'll talk about it. If the place has an aroma, they will, of course, talk about it. A potential buyer is often the harshest critic you will ever encounter.

DID YOU KNOW...
A scent can also represent one of the Five Elements. For example, *Fire* can be increased using the aromas of ginger, jasmine, and lemon.

You must believe that every choice you make has a MAJOR impact and that every item or color you have in your home is open to scrutiny. Is this fair? NO! I know what you are thinking . . . "Well, they aren't buying my furniture", or "They can paint the house any color they want . . . what I've chosen is no big deal ", or "They should be able to look beyond such things like the smell of my pet". I don't disagree that they **should** be able to look beyond these things, but the fact is . . . they don't! People will judge everything about your home, fairly or unfairly, during the period your house is on the market. Life isn't always fair, but it helps when you know the rules.

Let's examine a den with a brick fireplace and three large, consecutive windows, situated in the back of the house in the left corner. In the next chapter, you will learn that this area (or quadrant) of the house has Wood represented as its primary element. So we definitely want Wood to be solidly present. If the floors in this area are hardwood, we may immediately have enough of this element. Probably the room also has wood furniture. If so, we almost certainly have this element taken care of . . . and now may have too much wood. There are two ways to handle the idea of "too much" of a particular element. *We could take out some of the wood (or the element in question) from the room OR we could "minimize" the effect by bringing another element that neutralizes it.*

We certainly aren't going to take up the hardwood floors, but we could pull out some or all of that wood furniture. But often, a client likes the furniture and wants to keep it . . . so we use what has been called the "**Destructive Cycle**" or the "**Diminishing Cycle**" to accomplish the trick.

This cycle goes like this:

- Metal is "melted" by Fire

- Wood is "cut" by Metal

- Earth is "penetrated" by trees (Wood)

- Water is "absorbed" by Earth

- Fire is "extinguished" by Water

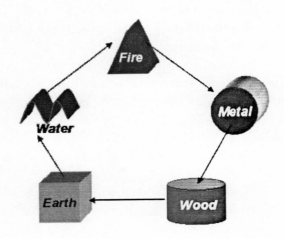

Cycles of Change
Destructive Cycle

Using this philosophy, to decrease the Wood element and its influence in a room, we could bring in more of the Metal element to combat the imbalance. We might include some spheres or globes, hang a modern piece of art with circles in it, add some metal furniture or sculptures, or bring in the colors that give us the metal element . . . white, silver, and gold. As in all "cures", monitor the changes. Remember, start small, monitor, and then increase if necessary.

Suppose a room seems to have too much Fire? As noted above, Fire is "extinguished" by Water. Of course we could get rid of some of the symbols, shapes, or colors that represent Fire, but if we like these things as they are, we will want to use the "Destructive Cycle" to accomplish this task. We could bring in a water fountain, an aquarium, a picture of the beach or a peaceful lake, paint a wall blue, or add some black leather furniture. A mirror also gives us Water, and is often a popular choice for enhancing this element.

Let's go back to our den. We decided earlier that the den has too much Wood. So we make the decision to paint the mantle of the fireplace white (Metal), add a globe, and change out one of the picture frames from wood to metal. This may be all we need to do get rid of this out-of-balance situation. We further notice that the fireplace gives us enough of the Fire element and with the walls painted a pale yellow, we have Earth, but Water is missing all together. So to add a touch of Water, we have a lot of options . . . perhaps we decide to just add a great sounding water fountain. We start to monitor our feelings and those of our guests, and possibly make a few adjustments. This is how the Five Elements can be manipulated in an environment.

Now suppose you don't like water fountains (or their sound). What can we do in this situation? Again, we have two choices:

1) **We could add the missing element**
2) **Or we could use the "Creative Cycle" to bring in the missing element**

The Creative or Constructive Cycle is a way to add the element without using the element. For example, a person may notice that a room needs the Fire element, but absolutely hates the color red, and doesn't what to use a pyramid or triangle in the decorations. The den in question has a fireplace, but what if our room didn't? That's where the Creative Cycle comes into play! This cycle goes like this:

- Wood is "fuel" for Fire
- Fire "creates" ash or Earth
- Earth "grows" or gives birth to Metal
- Metal when "heated" sufficiently becomes liquid like Water
- Water makes Wood "grow"

So, if we needed to add some Wood to an environment we could just add wood, but we note that "Water makes Wood grow", so we may prefer to just add more Water to accomplish the same end product. Or, if we needed some Metal we could up the amount of Earth.

The great thing about Feng Shui is that it gives us ways to get the balance we need without having to remove something we like (or have to keep) or requiring us to add something we really don't care for (like the color red).

Before we leave this chapter, understand that The Five Elements are a powerful way to get a balanced environment. We need to start by practicing our "Feng Shui eyes" in order to see what our environments are lacking. In Chapter 7 we will use another major tool to diagnose a floor plan. This will allow us to find the dominant element in each area of the house, and use that information to make additional changes.

As we increase our knowledge base, we need to take this information, and do something about it. We have already learned to reduce our clutter, increase the "flow" of our rooms, plan for color, and evaluate the presence of the Five Elements. We will add additional tools that allow us to play the real estate game . . . and win!

Points to Remember:

1) Each room in your house has a primary element
2) Each room in your house needs to have some of each element
3) Many rooms or environments in the United States are missing several of the elements . . . often Fire, Water, and Metal

4) If you don't like to take away or add something to a room, just use one of the cycles to accomplish the change
5) Many homes in western society have too much Wood and Earth

Frequently Asked Questions:

What constitutes a balance with respect to the Five Elements?
As you will see in the next chapter, the actual position of a room in a house has a lot to do with which element is dominant. The back right hand corner is Earth, the front left corner is Earth also, the middle of the front of the house is Water, and far back left corner is Wood. Once you finish Chapter 7, it will be easier how to start choosing the elements for a section of your environment.

Why should we make small changes first when trying to get a balance?
Often a person will go too far, and create more problems for an environment. You will eventually get better and better at making the correct changes and the amounts, but especially starting off . . . go slow.

Isn't neutral what sells homes?
Not really! What sells one home over another often comes down to the little things. It always amazes me when a better furnished house will finish first even though the other house down the street has the floor plan they initially thought was perfect for their family. Or a home that looks barren and cold is eliminated even though it is a great buy in a great neighborhood. Emotion sells a lot of homes every year!

Is the "Destructive Cycle" bad?
Not at all! It is just another way to manipulate the energy in a room. It is a powerful way to achieve "good" Chi.

"I love to think of nature
as an unlimited broadcasting station,
through which God speaks to us every hour,
if we only will tune in"

George Washington Carver
1864-1943

CHAPTER 7

The Magical Energy Template

One day Lisa, a local realtor, contacted a Feng Shui Consultant to come out to a vacant home she had listed seventeen weeks earlier. Not an easy sell to begin with, she felt her job had gotten even more difficult because the owners had finally moved their belongings out of state to their new home. They felt they had no real choice even though she had told them that a furnished home was easier to sell.

With her owners making it clear that they were going to start interviewing other agents if they didn't have a contract within the next month, Lisa knew she had to look into another approach. Her fellow agent, Samantha, had experienced success using a Feng Shui expert on two very difficult listings the past year, and Lisa decided to get her number and call.

The Feng Shui Practitioner met Lisa out at her vacant home, and first went over the basics to the philosophy. After spending the first 15 minutes giving Lisa an idea of what was going to take place, she disappeared for an hour walking the house and taking notes.

When she came back outside, Lisa was waiting for her and asked her if she had found anything. The consultant answered in the affirmative, and told her to meet her at the house the next day at noon. She had prepared a report that gave Lisa specific advice on how to enhance the Career, Helpful People, and Fame areas inside by just adding a few props. She was told that these areas alone would often make a home sink or swim, and had to be corrected.

Following her advice, Lisa brought in a couple of items, made sure the yard sign was moved to the preferred location, and had the house thoroughly cleaned. One week later, the house had been shown much more often, and more importantly, her homeowners had received an offer that they were very pleased with!

One of the most powerful and useful tools in your Feng Shui toolbox is an energy template or map called the **BAGUA**. Although the Bagua is usually presented as a regular octagon (all eight sides are equal), it actually molds itself to the house plan by usually becoming more of a rectangle. There are NINE areas or quadrants called **GUAS**. Each Gua represents a particular life event or situation. These quadrants are named:

CAREER

HELPFUL PEOPLE or TRAVEL

CHILDREN or CREATIVITY

RELATIONSHIP or MARRIAGE

FAME

WEALTH

FAMILY

KNOWLEDGE or SPIRTUALITY

HEALTH

These locations in your home or office are found by placing this energy map over top of the floorplan with the Bagua aligned with the front door . . . which we earlier called *The Mouth of Chi.*

Every person's front door or entrance comes into one of three locations. Those locations are Career, Helpful People, or Knowledge. Many homes have their entrance in the middle of the home, and people enter in the *Career* gua. But not all front doors are in the middle of the house. When aligning the floor plan, if the entrance is on the right, it comes through the *Helpful People* Gua, and if on the left, the entrance is in the *Knowledge* area.

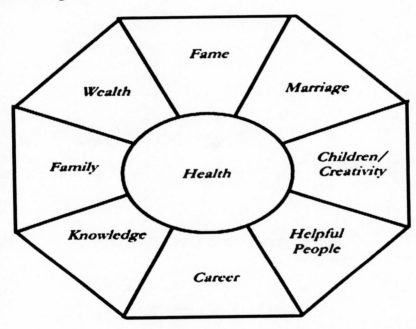

Most houses are NOT a perfect fit for an octagonal shape, so the different areas mold into more of a rectangle. With respect to a lot of the new floor plans which have "U" shape homes and "L" shape homes, there are many areas absent, called "missing corners", or many "additions". Additions are nothing to be feared, as they are quite positive and just enhance a Gua by making it bigger and more powerful. But we must address missing corners. If your home has a missing corner, don't fret. A missing corner can be cured quite easily by squaring it off . . . adding a plant, statue, flag, or something else that makes it become symbolically a "whole figure". Often rows of potted plants can be used to further aid in creating a whole figure or a rectangle.

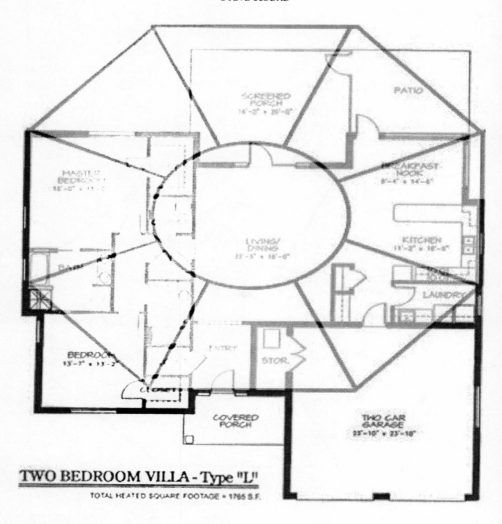

TWO BEDROOM VILLA - Type "L"

TOTAL HEATED SQUARE FOOTAGE = 1765 S.F.

So, the first thing to do is to align the Bagua over the top of your house floor plan as accurately as possible, then find the area where the front door enters. While you can start with the any area, it helps to do it in an organized fashion.

Usually the first area you enter is the *Career* area, located in the middle of the front of your home. Often it is in a foyer, but not always. As we learned in Chapter Six, an area has a primary element, and the Career area's dominant area is *Water*. So we need to strongly consider the Water element, as well as all sorts of symbolism for water when preparing this area to its best Feng Shui advantage.

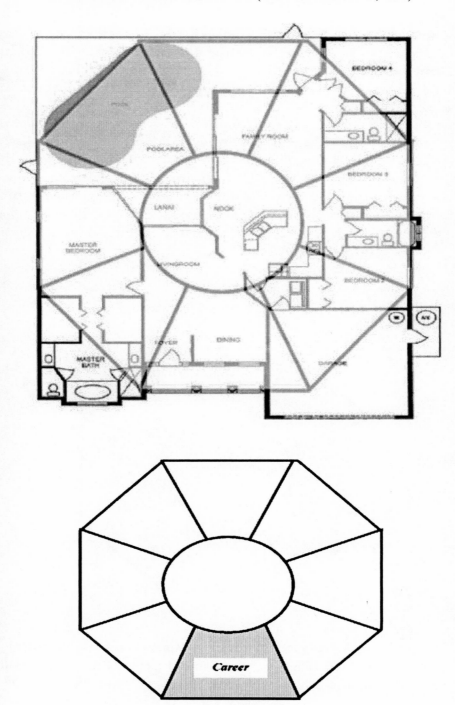

As we have already learned, the best colors for this area of the house are dark blue and black . . . in Chapter Six, we identified these colors as "Water" colors. One of these colors might be optimum, but if that isn't possible, you can, as you already know, use other means to bring in Water. A mirror, although not facing the front door, would be great, but a nice seascape would also work, and meandering shapes in a rug also pull it off well. The Career area of an environment needs to be enhanced for any individual who wants to start a new career, receive a promotion, or get a raise. For real estate purposes, the Career area is one of the three **MOST** important areas to dress up, so don't skimp when working on this area of a home for sale! For example, don't paint the walls a Yin color when selling; instead, use a slightly Yang color and bring in the dominant Water element with accessories. Keep it light and bright!

Moving in a counter clockwise direction, we enter the *Helpful People* (or Travel) area. This is also one of the three MOST important areas to be sure to work on strongly.

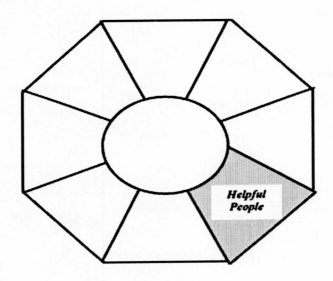

We all need helpful people in our lives to achieve our goals and to enjoy life. With respect to selling a home, the role of Helpful People is especially important. We need to work with people in a real estate transaction like

buyers, buyer agents, appraisers, inspectors, lawyers, and loan officers.
Anyone who has sold a house before probably knows how easily a real estate
deal can go haywire. There can be a problem with the loan or with a bad
home inspection. A lawyer or paralegal can be difficult or unhelpful, and of
course there may be a real problem negotiating a contract with the buyers
and their agent. We need help to make this sale go through without major
problems. The *Helpful People* primary element is *Metal* . . . so anything
white, silver, or gold is good. Items that have metal in them work, too. This
area is fine with a mixture of colors, so we can use a flower arrangement with
multi-colored flowers here. This is the place to put your house brochures
and your business cards. This area is an attractor for buyers; we need to pay
a lot of attention to this area inside and out. When you lay the Bagua over
the entire lot pay careful attention to the Helpful People area both inside
and out!

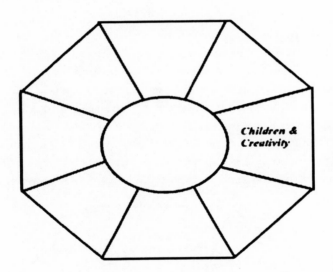

The next area is the **Children** or **Creativity** area, and the primary element
is also *Metal*. If this neighborhood and house will probably be attracting a
family with kids, then this area should also be worked on. If this home is
likely to attract more of an empty-nester couple, at least keep the area very
clean, add some white and/or metal if needed, especially make sure it is totally
clear of clutter.

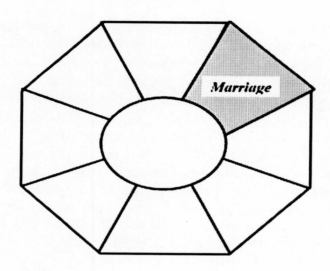

The **Marriage** or **Relationship** corner can also be quite important if a couple or young single person will probably be the buyer. The element here is *Earth*, so make sure your Earth element is present and healthy. The colors associated with this area are pink, red, and white. Even though pink can be a problem for some males, adding it in small doses can be powerful. Just don't forget, a little goes a long way. Because this is the marriage and relationship area, pairs of things are also auspicious. You may not need to go as far as a pair of stuffed monkeys or doves, but "pairs" will work magic in this location. Dressing this location up appropriately can give buyers a sub-conscious impression that their current or potential relationship is going to be positive.

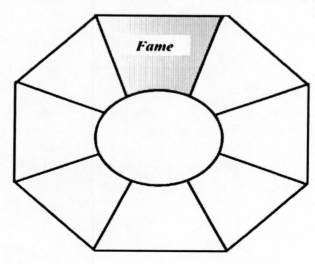

As we continue counter clockwise, we arrive at the **Fame** area. For the sale of a home, Fame is BIG! For a real estate agent, your reputation and acknowledgement are important with this sale, as well as many others to come. The element associated with this area is *Fire*, and therefore the primary color is **Red**. This area, located in the middle of the house at the back, is necessary for the overall balance of the house. *This is one of the three most important quadrants to enhance in any of your listings.* This is a good area to place awards, use the pyramid and triangle shapes, and introduce the colors of red, purple, and green, with an emphasis on red. Just remember . . . at little red goes a long way!

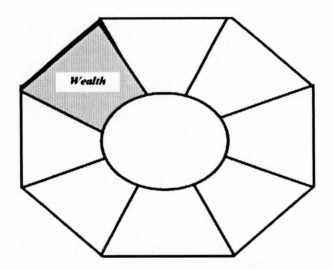

The *Wealth* corner is to the back left, and its associated element is *Wood*. The primary color is purple, but red and green can work well here. While plants can be extremely helpful anywhere in the house that is for sale, definitely place one here. As usual, don't go crazy . . . one or two plants are best. Try to stay away from plants that have pointy or sharp leaves, especially any type of cactus. These types of plants give off a reduced feeling of comfort for our visitors. We want as much "comfort" as possible in our listings!

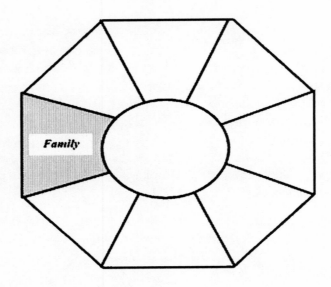

The **Family** corner is next, and its element is also *Wood*. Green is the best color to show here, but some blue can work here also. For the sale of a home, this area is NOT as important as many others. But, once again, follow the normal rules: very clean, no clutter, and a nice aroma.

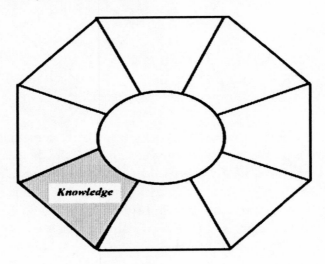

The **Knowledge** Gua comes up next, and is also less important to worry about when selling a home. Dark Blue is the primary color, but black and green can work. Follow the rules!

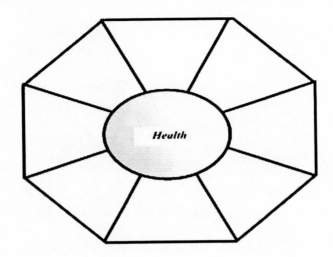

We now will proceed to the center of the house. This is the **Health** area, and as a result, is very important. The element associated with the Health area is *Earth*, and the colors are yellow and earth tones. The Health Gua is the center of a house both figuratively and literally. If a person's health is not addressed appropriately, then all of the other "spokes" of this wheel will not be as efficient. Please follow the rules as before, but pay special attention if a bathroom or kitchen is in this location.

In Feng Shui, it is often said that there is never a good place for a bathroom. If all locations are bad, then the middle of the house is probably the worst. If this is the case, be sure to keep the door closed at all times. Also hang a crystal just inside the front door to reflect Chi away from the drains and back out to the rest of the house. Any time a bathroom, or kitchen can be seen immediately when entering the front door, we have a problem that needs to be addressed. It is critical that this area be pristine and always free from clutter and distraction.

DID YOU KNOW...
Depending on the school of Feng Shui you consider, the energy template may be aligned with respect to compass direction. Black Hat always aligns with the front door.

Don't forget to place this magical energy template over top of your home floorplan aligned with the front door. It doesn't matter if you use the front door infrequently. Over the course of the last few chapters, you now have several tools you can use to gather information to create change. These tools include 1) *clutter control*; 2) *using Yin and Yang to emphasize the purpose of rooms*; 3) *The Five Elements*; and finally, 4) *the Bagua*.

Points to Remember:

1) There are Nine specific areas in any environment
2) The Bagua is an octagon, but when applied to a house, it often becomes a rectangle.
3) Each area is important when selling a home, but three areas are especially important. These three are: **Career**, **Helpful People**, and **Fame**.
4) All homes do **NOT** appeal to everybody. Determine the areas to enhance, based on the "market" for the home. If the home is perfect for a family, enhance the **Children** area. If the house is more for a couple or single person, the **Relationship** area would be better to work on.
5) The Bagua is another way to get information to improve the Feng Shui of an environment.

Frequently Asked Questions:

Is the octagon an important figure?
Yes it is. All whole shapes are auspicious in Feng Shui. The octagon and circle are especially powerful, but a square is also good. If it was possible, all houses would be these shapes (or a rectangle) . . . but of course they are not. Many of today's houses are irregular in shape, with "missing corners".

Is a missing corner harmful?
It can be if not "cured". Always think about "squaring" it off by the use of plants, statues, etc. A missing corner can mean we have less support or positive energy for the specific life situation associated with the area, for example, Wealth.

I've noticed on my home I have a huge area missing. Is this possible?
If the area missing is over ½ of the side of the house, you actually have an extension and not a missing corner. This is actually good!

If my Knowledge area is in the garage, do I have a problem?
No . . . just keep this area uncluttered and as clean as possible.

You have said that for a real estate agent the three most important sections are Fame, Helpful People, and Career. Should I stop with these three with my listings?
It would be more powerful if you consider what type of a buyer would most probably buy this house, and work on one more area, in addition to these three. For example: if this is a child friendly neighborhood, work on the Children/Creativity section.

One of my listings has its Marriage corner in a screened porch. What do you recommend?
First clean and un-clutter. Secondly, focus on the "pairs" metaphor for relationships. You can add a pair of matching candles, lights, or knick knacks of some sort . . . preferably in pink, white or red.

I understand for a real estate agent that the Fame area is quite important. Any tips on how to highlight this area in my listings?
Use the color red in this area, and place one of your brochures in the area. You can use any thing else that represents your success, such as a newspaper article or advertisement. These objects do not have to be obvious or out in the open. You can hide them behind a photo or painting . . . or underneath a book.

"To most men their early home is no more than a
memory of their early years. The image is never marred.
There's no disappointment in memory,
and one's exaggerations are always on the good side."

George Eliot
1819-1880

CHAPTER 8

Making Sense of The Five Senses

A couple, Frank and Deanna Carson, had just flown in from California to look for a house. Frank had taken his dream job just days ago with a huge increase in salary. Neither of them wanted to leave southern California, but both knew this was a great opportunity for them. Deanna had been decorating their home in California for years using Feng Shui, and really believed in its many benefits. Frank had come to be a believer himself, as his business had gotten better and better. The Carsons wanted to be able to consult with a practitioner or a real estate agent with Feng Shui experience, so they got on the Internet to find the person to help them locate the right piece of real estate.

After searching, Deanna found a local practitioner who advertised the service of locating real estate that was "good" Feng Shui. His name was Allen, and after calling him one night, Deanna thought he could supply the kind of help they needed. With Allen's help, Deanna planned to narrow the search down to three homes, then get Frank involved to make the final decision. Their real estate agent didn't mind having Allen along when showing Deanna homes. It actually allowed her to more quickly weed out several properties the Carsons were unlikely to consider.

After three days of looking, Allen and Deanna had identified five homes that met most of the criteria. The first one was on a nice quiet street with little traffic and a private backyard with a protective cluster of trees behind the house. The inside was sort of choppy, but the kitchen was sunny and open and located in a good position. It felt pretty good, but Deanna was not totally sold . . . although she considered it a solid maybe.

The second home was on a dead-end street and had very little vibrant vegetation on the property. The house on the right was a 3-story home and seemed to tower over the home they were scheduled to see. They agreed that they would pass on looking at the inside of this home . . . as it had really bad Feng Shui going for it.

The next home was a nice one level with a well landscaped yard. Walking in, it felt slightly claustrophobic as the entry's door didn't open entirely all the way and it was not well lit. The house smelled a little. None of the team were quite sure what the aroma was, but it wasn't positive. They quickly took a look; although the floor plan was almost perfect, it didn't seem right.

The fourth home was gorgeous from the outside, but was on a busy street and while the team was visiting, several planes flew over at low altitudes. It was easy to make the assumption that this was a flight pattern for the airport a couple of miles away. Deanna loved the floor plan, but the noise was always present, and it didn't seem to be a good place to relax after a hard day at the office.

The last home was located in the back of a quiet neighborhood. It had lots of mature hardwood trees with abundant wild life. Squirrels, birds, and all types of insects seemed to happily go on about their business. Walking into the foyer was very pleasant. It was up beat and smelled like someone's grandmother has just baked some of those yummy oatmeal raisin cookies. Deanna automatically felt more comfortable and content. The natural light was abundant and the house was sparkling. A soft piece of classical music was playing in the background, and added to her peaceful feelings. Allen remarked about the positioning of the stove, the colors already in use in the master suite, and how the walkway meandered towards the front door.

Deanna knew she needed Frank to take a look at this one . . . it felt right on many levels!

Any good real estate agent, and for that matter any good salesman, needs to take into account senses other than sight. Sight is certainly a BIG factor for potential buyers, but the feelings they get from the other senses plays such a big role that you can easily lose the sale if one of these is not right. What if buyers walk into your listing and love the neighborhood, think the outside is gorgeous, the layout is perfect, location is five minutes to work, and their best friend is 3 doors down the block? Sure sale? Not if the house smells; when they walk into this home, that's a real turnoff! While some people can look beyond things, most buyers are driven by emotional response. Buyers also often lack creativity. They can't visualize their furniture in an empty home, can't imagine a different color on the living room wall, won't consider a home without a manicured lawn, or seem to get lost when anything funky shows up. They can't see that this house could be their home unless it closely matches what they think it should look like.

Many of the buyers you encounter are like this to some degree. How many? Well, my experience, and some data, gives a figure around 40 to 50 percent! And here's the scary part . . . this figure may be low. What I'm getting to is this . . . most buyers need help "seeing" the house. If the dining room is being used as a kid's play room, big problem. They may acknowledge that this room originally was a dining room, but when they think about the house later, what they will remember that it was lacking this important item. In my experience, buyers see lots of houses and don't remember each one really well . . . they just remember their impressions. They don't want to hear that this room COULD be a dining room; they want to see some attempt to show it. Without a table in the room, they begin to wonder if this room is too small for the table Mom gave them.

So what does any of this have to do with the five senses? Let's start with one of the five senses . . . *smell*. Depending on who you talk to, smell can represent from 10 to 30% of a person's opinion about an environment. According to recent research, the sense of smell is a primary factor in the human sensation of comfort, although compared to the senses of sight, hearing, and touch, scientists know relatively little about how humans smell and taste. Your sense of smell is a controlling key for your emotional responses to life. This is because the emotional part of your brain evolved from the part of the brain used to translate smells.

Even if only 10% of a person's reaction is based on smell, you do not want to take the chance of a bad smell ruining the opportunity to get an offer. As an experienced agent, you know that an offer—any offer—even if it is poor one, is priceless. An offer gives you a chance to negotiate, and often can be worked out. I always tell my homeowners to always be glad of getting an offer and don't get sensitive if it comes in low. This is a great opportunity to negotiate a deal you do want!

Smells have often derailed an offer or decreased a higher offer in real estate. We know this is true, but sometimes we are so focused on just the visual that we pass over it. I'm here to tell you . . . don't! Feng Shui takes the senses into account, and smells can be bad or good, Yin or Yang. In every home you have for sale, find out if a home regularly has the smell of smoke, curry, cabbage, fish, or any moldy, pungent smell, and get rid of it before you ever show it the first time. People who live in a house do not smell the offending aroma, so they really need your help. They need you to be upfront with them, which may mean you need to tell them their home smells bad.

Some people are very positive about particular aromas that are not universally liked by the majority of people. As with anything, we need to appeal to the majority . . . but we also need to be consistent. Save the "specialty" aroma for a home that's not for sale, and focus on a consistent positive aroma throughout the house. What I mean by consistent is that often you will use the same aroma throughout the house. It is poor thinking to have several smells going on, no matter how positive, in a house. I do think, with a 2-story or 1 ½ story home that you can make the downstairs more Yang, and the upstairs more Yin, and it can be powerful. BUT, what ever you do . . . the aroma has to be subtle and not over-powering like some perfumes or aftershave.

You may enjoy some smells or aromas that, on your opinion, are just great . . . like lavender. But lavender, although positive to some folks, is traditionally believed to be sleep-inducing, and for me, it is not a high ranking smell when trying to sell a home. Anything too sweet or perfumy is not a good choice. Some people like smells such as pine, rose, mint, and strawberry . . . but for me . . . the hands-down winners are **cinnamon** and **French vanilla**. If you only want to pick one smell that is prevalent in your home that is for sale, I'd pick one of these. Both of these smells are more Yang, but at the same time quite comforting.

Researchers have found that just having the aroma of cinnamon in a room reduces drowsiness, irritability, and the pain and frequency of headaches. Studies conducted at Sloan-Kettering found that people undergoing stressful medical tests responded positively to the smell of a vanilla-like fragrance, with 57% preferring it to other tested aromas. They concluded that, "vanilla, a homey scent which may remind people of food, may be a preferred scent" for most people. We know these smells, if not overpowering, can elicit memories of Grandma baking cookies. Since we want our buyers to think good thoughts, these create that atmosphere. I bet some of you have had your home seller bake some cookies before a showing or an open house. Why? Because it creates a positive backdrop that makes a person feel at home. And if you haven't let it sink in yet . . . we want people to feel at home, see themselves living here, knowing they will be REALLY comfortable.

DID YOU KNOW...
When selling a home, most people only consider the visual when showing their home to potential buyers. Depending on which study you look at, you could be missing 25% to 35% of what an individual takes in as positive or negative.

While we want some compatibility in aroma, another choice is to give a different smell in the kitchen, and possibly the bathrooms. Nothing gives the feeling of cleanliness like that of citrus . . . especially lemon. We will talk about this more in Chapter 9: *The Kitchen*. As stated, my favorite aromas are cinnamon, French vanilla, and lemon when trying to get a home sold. There are three ways I'd consider using these fragrances in a two-story home:

- Two different scents, with cinnamon downstairs and French vanilla upstairs

- Only one scent, with either French vanilla or cinnamon on both floors

- Or finally, pick cinnamon or French vanilla for both floors, and change up with a citrus scent in the kitchen and bathrooms.

I also love citrus for an office, because we want one thing . . . activity. The last thing we want in a work environment is for people to feel drowsy, so the more Yang the better! But in a house, we have areas that we want to either be slightly more Yin or almost totally Yin, such as the bedrooms, or areas where we relax. Now certainly, if you want to create your own heaven on earth for yourself, a favorite aroma, subtly used, is positive. But we are attempting to sell a home, so we must appeal to the majority of noses!

A third sense whose importance we often overlook is sound. In *"The Hidden Messages in Water"*, Dr. Masaru Emoto, a renowned Japanese scientist, did experiments on the impact of sound on water crystals that were truly amazing. Since water makes up over 75% of the earth, and of our body composition, his research can suggest some parallels for us. Dr. Emoto studied the formation of water crystals in a very cold room, while applying different stimuli to them. He has astounded the world by photographing the behavior of one of our most important resources. Music, which is a form of vibration, is a powerful producer of emotions in us. His experiments with music show just how powerful! When he applied soft classical music such as Tchaikovsky's Swan Lake, Mozart's Symphony No. 40, or Beethoven's Symphony No. 6 he produced amazingly beautiful, full formed crystals. When he played heavy metal music loaded with angry and vulgar lyrics, the crystals were very deformed! His experiments with types of music like The Beatles' *Yesterday* formed lovely formations, but the use of Rap or songs full of despair immediately gave the opposite effect.

We know music has powerful appeal to our emotions, both positively and negatively. Music can also have a powerful effect on the sale of a home. If you pick something that is positive, peaceful, and beautiful it can help transform a buyer's visit into an exceptional experience. But if you don't consider the auditory sense of the potential visitor, you are potentially setting yourself up for another month or two of making those #$@$& beds! This is especially important if you live on a busy street, have noisy neighbors, or an occasional plane flies over. The soothing sounds of the music can mask the negative noise, while creating the right atmosphere for your potential buyers. More importantly, music can affect a buyer's willingness to make a purchase. In a survey of 774 shoppers at a large retail center, professors of marketing at Rutgers-Camden found that impulsive shoppers—characterized as those who make unplanned purchases more often than so-called contemplative buyers—spend more money when pleasant music is playing in the background. Contemplative shoppers, on the other hand, tend to spend more money when a pleasant odor is in the background.

Now, we are left with just two senses—taste and touch/feel. Certainly taste and feel are down the list of potential turn-offs for a buyer, but even they, at times, can come into play. You certainly could consider putting out some fresh cookies and lemonade for the potential buyer to enjoy; hopefully, they will stay in your beautiful kitchen and ponder the many benefits of your home. You want to make sure that if they run their hands over the mantle over the fireplace, or the counters in the kitchen, or the marble vanities in the bathrooms that they are not dirty and dusty.

The *temperature* is also an important part of the sense of feel. At what temperature do you keep your thermostat when your home is being shown? I remember showing a vacant home in the winter, where the homeowner did not believe that heating all of that empty space was really necessary. Think how poorly this home came off to prospective buyers with temperatures never rising above 45 to 50 degrees. Do you think that they felt like staying and pondering this home? Of course not! In the summer . . . a nicely cooled home is very refreshing and allows a buyer to stay in your home longer.

A homeowner needs to understand comfort and its relation to selling a home. A homeowner needs to develop an understanding that buyers will stay a little longer if everything feels right. There have been studies conducted to find out at what temperature a human being feels best. Best to do what? Well, if a person is just wanting to be comfortable during the winter months and not do anything very physical, a temperature of 71 to 74 degrees might be fine, but if they actually plan to move around a lot, a lower temperature is better . . . say 67 to 70 degrees. In the middle of a sweltering summer, anything over 74 inside is often a little uncomfortable for most people. What ever you do, make sure the temperature is in a range that is comfortable for the majority of people. In the winter, I would advocate you to keep the thermostat in a range no lower than 70 and no higher than 72. In the summer, make it equally refreshing by staying in the same range. If your home does not cool sufficiently, you may need to lower it slightly more.

Your buyers must come in and feel great being there! If they feel uncomfortable, they will be in a hurry to leave. A recent poll given on Google asked the following question: *"Which temperature range for the indoors do you find most comfortable?"* Out of a sample of 52 votes, 36 of the votes were for a range between 68 and 72 degrees. This backs up other studies into optimum temperatures for productivity in an office. If your homeowners are insisting on saving on the utility bills when attempting to sell their home, make them understand that they are actually costing themselves money by being bull-headed! Each of the five senses gives people information about the environment . . . it can be good or bad information. Make sure it is all good!

Let's finish this chapter talking about our visual sense one more time, specifically in regard to color. Possibly nothing will impact your showing more than your use of color. Different colors elicit different emotions. As a real estate agent (or homeowner), you need to know what colors push people's emotions and where to use those colors for maximum positive effect. We have already mentioned colors a great deal in *Chapter Six: The Five Elements* and *Chapter Seven: The Bagua*. We will now attempt to put it all together for you within the next couple of pages. Many folks seem to be color blind when decorating their homes. Let's face it, some colors go with particular colors better than with others! Some colors in some rooms make no sense at all! Our society has got it mixed up with respect to neutrality!

When you look examine a **Color Wheel** at your local paint store, you can begin to see what colors are complimentary, and which ones just look strange. The primary colors are red, blue, and yellow. The secondary colors are green, orange, and purple. Secondary colors are combinations of the primary colors. You some times hear about tertiary colors. These are primary colors in combination with a closest secondary color . . . for example, red-orange. We can often use the color wheel to decide what our theme will be, and which colors are likely to complement each other. But there is more to it than just how they look together. Colors affect our moods!!

This is a very important thing for you to have sink in. Each room in the house you are attempting to sell has a specific mood associated with it . . . our job is to help present the right one. For example: we do not want the mood in our master bedroom to be one of heated conversation or increased energy. Our bedrooms are places for rest and relaxation. If we fail to set this mood for our potential buyers, you are confusing them.

As I've stated before, you must lead the buyer . . . you want them to follow your "path" for viewing the home, and you want them to respond to each room as expected. Therefore, each and every room in your listing must give off the correct vibrations. The direct impact of color is easy to understand. Some colors make us happy or energized. Some colors are distracting. Some colors even make us depressed. The relationship between color and a human's energy is powerful. Color influences us from morning to when we go to bed. The minute we open our eyes in the morning, we see the color of the ceiling. When we drive to work, we see colors of all sorts that create a feeling. Our own Chi is affected by our reaction to the different colors we see on the way to work, at work, at the restaurant we have lunch, on the way home, at the entrance of our home, and when we sit down in our favorite chair what pictures or walls we are facing. Color really has a lot to do with how we are participating with life and how we are succeeding in life.

If we want a particular reaction from a buyer, we need to make sure it is the one we are really after, and not let it fall for chance. By choosing the right accessories and colors in the home we are selling, we can hopefully manipulate their overall reaction to their visit. We have one chance to impress. We have one opportunity to get on their "final cut" list. Here is a compilation of reactions to particular colors. By considering these reactions to color, along with The Five Element balance we are trying to achieve, Yin and Yang, and the Bagua, we can receive the best effect from our showings.

- RED—symbolizes passion, happiness, and attention

- ORANGE—stimulates appetite and conversation

- YELLOW—increases energy

- GREEN—encourages emotional and mental growth

- BLUE—produces peace and relaxation

- PINK—promotes affection, love and togetherness

- PURPLE—is spiritual and represents wealth and success

- WHITE—represents purity and cleanliness

- BLACK—encourages independence and can be depressing

Passive colors like blue, green, and purple are considered cool colors and can create a calm atmosphere. Active colors like red, orange, and yellow are considered warm colors and tend to stand out and dominant a room. Neutral colors like beige, brown, gray, and white are merely a combination of active and passive. Consider your choices strongly, and recommend your seller repaint where necessary. Although painting is one of the least expensive changes to make to a home, many buyers come into a home, see a room painted a color which either confuses or irritates them, and they decide it is too much trouble to buy a house they will need to repaint. Although this kind of decision process is frustrating for realtors and home sellers alike, it happens way too often.

If your seller is reluctant to repaint, consider other possibilities. When dealing with a strong, active color, consider leaving only one wall with this color, and tone down the color on the other walls. With an extremely strong color like red, one wall may be more than enough. Two walls or more . . . no way! If you want to use a variation of red on all walls, fine . . . but tone it down with white, gray, or brown to get less of a reaction. Rose, burgundy, or shades of pink may have some of the power of red, but they generally are more pleasing to the majority of potential buyers. Let me again make a point about use of room and Yin/Yang. Don't confuse the buyer by making the bedroom too Yang (red, orange, etc.) and a den more Yin (dark blue, forest green, etc.). If these are the colors you prefer, great . . . but tone them down so that you have more of a balanced mix of Yin and Yang when selling.

Points to Remember:

1) A house that is for sale needs to appeal to a buyer's five senses.
2) After visual, smell will negatively effect a potential buyer's first impression the most.

3) Consider using smells that evoke happy feelings of the past . . . like grandmother's cookies.
4) Don't go overboard with changing the aromas from room to room.
5) Cinnamon and French vanilla have proven to be good choices for a home for sale.
6) A great addition, if necessary, is the smell of citrus in a kitchen.
7) The wrong sound can make a buyer turn right around and leave.
8) Certain types of music (soft classical, soft jazz, etc.) can make the experience more positive for a buyer
9) Consider taste and especially feel when selling a home.
10) Color can make or break a sale . . . give it a lot of thought.

Frequently Asked Questions:

My homeowner is adamant about keeping the lights off and the temperature down when he is at work. It is in the middle of the winter. Any suggestions?
Get out a calculator and a piece of paper. Draw a line down the middle of the paper, and label one column with utilities off and the other staying in the house for an extra month. Compile the so called "savings" for him to compare. If need be, take it out another month or two. He'll get the idea about how stupid it really is to save pennies a day when he could stop paying all of those monthly bills . . . especially the mortgage.

When I walk up to this listing I have, before I even get inside, I can smell cigarette smoke. Is this a major reason this home won't sell?
You bet ya!! Especially now, smoke is a major turn-off to most people. You have to get rid of the smell! You can't let a perspective buyer fully acknowledge that the current owner is a smoker. It smells bad, but it also is a health risk. You need to talk with them and urge them strongly that they must change their habit of smoking inside for a while and get rid of the smell immediately, or risk staying on the market forever.

I can't smell my pets. Do you really think anyone else does?
Trust me . . . if you have pets . . . there is a smell that you have just gotten used to. Many buyers have an aversion to pet smells, pet fur, or just pets themselves. Some people won't buy a home where pets have been kept, citing allergies or other concerns. Don't throw up a sign that says "pets on the premises". Remove your pets from the home during showings, pick up food dishes, take the cat

box with you if necessary, spray the house thoroughly to remove pet orders, and come up with some way that a looker won't think about your pets.

You are big on sound. What else can you tell me about this sense?
There are sounds outside your house right now that are either positive to your sale or negative. Do you live on a busy road (or off an interstate)? Is a school one block away? Does the airport use this area for one of their main landing routes? Are there barking dogs next door? It is hard to mask these sounds, but some of us have no alternative. Music can help alleviate the harshness of this problem for you also. Soft, positive music sets a mood inside your listing. Nature sounds, such as birds, can send very calming feelings to a buyer. Use sound in all of your listings!

My owner likes it hot in the summer. He has air conditioning, but does not want to use it. OK?
Not really!!! If it is 90 degrees outside, and a buyer walks into this house, he or she will be uncomfortable and disappointed by not becoming refreshed when entering. The buyer also may think thoughts like this: "maybe they don't have AC" or "the AC is probably not working, and they don't maintain this home well". You must make them understand, that during this period we are putting on a show. It is a production to get the best possible offer for their most prized possession. The homeowner's preference, at this time, is less important!

"A hundred men may make an encampment, but it takes
A women to make a home"

Chinese Proverb

CHAPTER 9

The Kitchen

In Feng Shui, the kitchen is at the top of the list for rooms that have to look amazing when trying to sell a home. A poorly organized, or even worse, a messy kitchen can and will stop potential buyers in their tracks. Even if the buyer is not especially interested in cooking . . . the kitchen has to look the part. Our society has become a fast food feast. We order more and more takeout and delivery than ever, but it doesn't matter. Although our kitchens are often more about how we serve the "takeout" than about how we prepare it, buyers want the kitchen to suggest they could be a gourmet cook if they only had the time.

You must make the kitchen shine! The kitchen, in Feng Shui, is where it all begins. Our health and daily nourishment come out of this area of the house, both figuratively and literally. It may be symbolic for some owners, but it still represents what makes everything else "work" in our lives . . . our health. When you look at the Bagua, every other life situation revolves around this one. If our health fails, other facets of our life will suffer. So we must seriously consider the make-up of the kitchen when working with Feng Shui.

It probably goes without saying, . . . the kitchen has to be . . . clean . . . clean . . . clean!! A serious buyer will take one look at a filthy kitchen, figure you probably deal with the rest of the house just as poorly, and will move on to the next home. Why give them any excuse. As I told you in another chapter, buyers are looking for a reason to say "NO"! Don't give it to them. Pull up your sleeves and make your kitchen sparkle; make it look like it has never been used. Get out those gloves and cleaning materials and make it look and smell like new!

Even if the kitchen is clean, a disorganized kitchen sends all the wrong messages to a potential buyer. It really makes them think on all levels, that your home is not going to move them towards an easier, healthier life. Clutter, which has already been talked about in depth, is a killer on a conscious and subconscious level. Kitchens attract clutter like no other room in the home. Everything in the house is NOT off-limits, as far as the buyers are concerned. As a realtor, make sure your client knows the buyers will get down and dirty to make sure your home meets their standards. They will look in the cabinets. They will look under the sink. They may even look in the refrigerator, and they probably will open the oven. Invasion of privacy? Not if the house is on the market! So pushing the clutter under the sink or in the pantry is NOT the right solution.

All of these impressions build up the buyer's final feelings on whether the kitchen, fairly or not, matches up. And once again, don't get caught up in the idea that many young buyers eat out, so the kitchen doesn't really matter. The kitchen easily could make up their minds right away. So we need to get extremely organized in here. As in all rooms, get rid of everything never or all most never used. Pack it up. Store it away. Give it away . . . just do it. This motto, throughout the entire house, will make you lots of money and less time on the market. So, starting with the cabinets, move out 50% or more of the "stuff" but only after you take *everything* out and clean like a fiend. After doing the cabinets, do the exact same thing with the pantry. A pantry is almost hallowed ground with buyers; you can NEVER have too much storage space! If your pantry is small, you need to give the illusion of space, by pulling everything off the shelves, cleaning it deeply, and putting back only the bare essentials. Now when I say put it back, I mean put it back in a "different" way! Have all labels pointing outward in the same direction, and line things up according to size. This gives them the idea that you are a "nut", but a "nut" that takes care of every little detail! Exactly the kind of person a buyer wants to find. They begin thinking *"This house is going to be so easy to live in . . . it will probably run itself and I'll have lots of time to go play golf!*

This is a good time to bring up smell again. The kitchen can NOT smell like last night's cabbage or curry or fish or whatever meal was served! Sellers often remark, *"well, they just have to understand that someone lives here"*. NO, they DON'T!! If the seller wants to play this card, they need to be prepared to sit on the house two to three months longer. Is that worth it? So as I said last chapter, smell is EXTREMELY important, and never more than in the kitchens and bathrooms.

A GREAT smell for a kitchen is one of **citrus**. Citrus just seems to give off the idea of cleanliness. Now I'm a great believer in one smell on the first floor, subtle, but obvious . . . but if you break this rule anywhere . . . this is definitely the place. Every other day, grind a small piece of lemon in your garbage disposal. This will keep down those offending odors that keep coming back to haunt us. If you are doing the kitchen with this aroma, use citrus cleaning supplies, a "stick-up" with this aroma, or a citrus kitchen spray and spray lightly before a showing. Consider effusion fragrance lamps that eliminate odor in the air while cooking. Don't forget, the buyer will be looking in drawers, cabinets, ovens, and refrigerators . . . so consider a quick spray in these areas as well.

The refrigerator must be uncluttered even if it's not being sold along with the house. NEVER leave all those disgusting magnets, restaurant menus, newspaper coupons and reminder notes attached to the refrigerator. They look terrible, and once again, the kitchen leaves a cluttered impression regardless of the time the buyers spend in it. The top of the refrigerator needs a deep cleaning also, and if you put anything back . . . make it something simple—a plant may be fine. Organize the interior of your frig also. Get rid of that casserole that's been in there for two weeks, throw out old veggies, and make it look spacious. I know you're not selling it, but you are selling this house. How the house comes off at every turn directly affects the buyers' perception of how you take care of the "old homestead". After spending time and effort to make the house shine, don't give the buyer a different feeling when they open the refrigerator door . . . clean it up inside, too!

The stove is very important. The stove, especially the burners, represent wealth, success, and health in Feng Shui. The burners all need to be used on a continuing basis. Don't favor one burner over the other. The burners all need to be cleaned thoroughly and have the pans shine! A stove is a good place for crumbs, food, and dust to collect . . . run a moist towel over it before a showing. It must sparkle during showings. Clean the oven and make it shine, especially if the oven is not self-cleaning. After cleaning, a silicone ovenliner can help keep it sparkling; the spills just wipe off. Just don't forget to wipe them up.

DID YOU KNOW...
The kitchen often makes or breaks a sale. When selling a home, the whole house should be given a deep cleaning...but especially the kitchen and the bathrooms!

A kitchen's countertops are important for many reasons. A countertop without clutter shows off the "space" available to put the buyer's "stuff". Advise the sellers to pack away or give away everything off the counters, other than essentials. Yes, I understand the toaster and coffeepot are necessary to getting started each morning, but I'd prefer that they be placed in a drawer or cabinet where they are still accessible if really needed. Today's countertops are often works of art . . . specialty laminate, solid surface, or granite. Covering them up doesn't make sense even if clutter were not an issue. Show them off! The counters, in a perfect world, would be spacious, with no clutter, spotlessly clean and smelling great.

There are many different types of floors in today's kitchen. They may be wood, ceramic tile, vinyl, and in some rare cases, carpet. Each of these floor coverings brings in a large amount of one of the Five Elements. There may be a need to create balance by counteracting an abundance of one of the elements. A kitchen floor may need a splash of color from a throw rug. A simple red, yellow, blue, or green floor rug can bring in an element that is lacking. But don't go crazy with little rugs—they can also create the impression of diminished space, and they cover up the floors.

Revisit the position of the kitchen with respect to the Bagua. Is the kitchen in the Children area? The dominant element here is *Metal*. Make sure it is present, and not over-shadowed by an element that reduces Metal. What if the kitchen is in the Wealth corner? Keep in mind the dominant element in the Wealth area is *Wood* and handle it the same way. The kitchen is NOT a place to fall asleep . . . so it definitely should be more Yang and needs to be seen and decorated that way. A kitchen can make or break a sale. You must give special attention to the kitchen when attempting to sell. As in all rooms, when preparing to show . . . don't forget to turn all lights on!

Points to Remember:

1) The kitchen is one of the rooms that will put a decision on placing an offer over the top.
2) Figure out where the kitchen lies with respect to the Bagua, and check to make sure the elements are balanced
3) Smell is extremely important in the kitchen.
4) Cleanliness is extremely important in the kitchen.
5) The kitchen is a Yang room . . . no dark blue walls here!
6) Lights on during showing!

Frequently Asked Questions:

Does it matter when I build a house where the kitchen is placed?
Actually, the best place for a kitchen is in the middle of a home—the Health area—and it is often where they are located. The kitchen should not be the first thing you see when entering a home, so it should NOT be in the front of the home.

I can't believe a potential buyer can not overlook my toaster on the counter?
Don't forget, when selling a home . . . it is an "artificial" setting. If you REALLY want to sell the home quickly and for probably more profit, you need to "fake it". Go visit some model homes in your area and make note of the staging in the kitchen. You will not see much clutter. The great thing about following this idea for Feng Shui is that we have less clutter and an easier flow of energy. Following these ideas are powerful on two fronts . . . common sense and Feng Shui!

I've always used lavender as the smell I have in my kitchen. I like it and so do my visitors. Why change?
Because lavender and other flowery smells are too "sweet" and therefore too Yin. Also these smells have a smaller number of people who like them!!! Keep the lavender for your new home, and cater to the majority of people who will be entering your home while it is on the market.

"There is no quiet place in the white man's cities, no place to
hear the leaves of spring or the rustle of insect's wings . . .

Chief Seattle
Chief of the Suquamps and Allied Tribes
(1786-1866)

CHAPTER 10

The Dining Room

Marty and Denise entertain a lot with dinner parties at their home. So when they began looking for a new home. it was really important that the dining room met their expectations. It had to be located near the front of the house and close to the kitchen, but they wanted it to easily handle their specially made dining room table with curved corners and eight chairs. If possible, they wanted the room to be located in the right front of the house, but were okay with it being on the left if necessary.

Natural light was important, but they also wanted to have a chandelier that brought in mood lighting and that helped cover the Five Elements. Too many of the houses they were seeing had the same old brass fixture. They were open to buying their own fixture if needed.

Marty and Denise figured they would have to paint the room, depending on its location, but were secretly hoping it was going to be workable so they could focus on other things first. Too many dining rooms were too Yin for their taste; they wanted an exciting environment; one that would promote interesting conversation during meals they shared with their many friends.

The dining room for the "typical" American family is never typical. The families of the 50's generally ate their meals together . . . especially the evening meal. In the 60's, with the advent of the infamous TV dinner, more folks ate around the television, if they ate together at all. As our society got out of sync with having a "family meal", the dining room was used less and less. Even today, a formal dining room is often way down the list of *must haves* for a home buyer. More and more new homes are offering more square footage in a "great room", acknowledging the trend away from sit down dinners. But some people still want a traditional dining room, especially people who entertain a lot. For some people, that one big Thanksgiving meal is important enough for them to continue planning for reasons to have the formal dining room. As with the kitchen, figure out which area of the Bagua the dining room is in and make a note.

If your listing has a formal dining room, you MUST make sure it looks the part. You must move out the office or the children's play room and make it look like a place where the All-American family sits and has meals together, even if it will never happen. Don't forget . . . we are selling dreams when we sell a home. Many people still remember shows like "Leave It to Beaver" or "The Cosby Show" and think . . . eventually I need to have a room set up like this so my family is not considered dysfunctional. A dining room needs to stand out as first a great place for the family and friends to get together, even if the buyer is a hermit.

Don't forget to use the Bagua. This information is always a big help in dictating certain important decisions about placement, additions, or subtractions

The dining room area can sometimes confuse buyers by being too Yin. Too many dining rooms in our society put people to sleep by having dark, drab colors. Make sure this room is more Yang, even if the current owners tend to use it for a quick pit stop in their own busy lives. We are selling a dream! Despite its current popularity, I'm not advocating you paint the walls red. This actually would be counterproductive. Did you know fast food restaurants like McDonalds use bright vibrant colors like red and yellow to stimulate your appetite and rush you out the door? They want you to come in, order a lot of food, eat it quickly, and leave. They want to "turn over" those tables as fast as possible . . . but don't forget the McSundae! So don't paint the walls bright yellow or red; do consider pale yellow, rose, and bright greens and blues. These colors will make you want to stay longer and "chew the fat". So we are after a color that is somewhat Yang, but not enough to blow you away.

One of nature's strongest Yang forces is lighting. Natural light is most favorable, and in every house it should be played up greatly, but often an environment needs extra help, especially during some seasons, to artificially illuminate. Light can be manipulated, just like energy, to create plays of shadow

DID YOU KNOW...
That certain colors and patterns make you eat faster and more. The colors of red and bright yellow and the patterns of circles and dots will make you gain more weight.

and color. It can transform the atmosphere of a room. One of the great advantages of lighting over other design aspects is its flexibility. Often, just by a flick of a switch, a room can be changed instantly.

When we consider the five elements, most dining rooms have too much *Wood* and probably *Earth*, so make sure the room is not totally out of balance by bringing in some *Water*, *Fire*, and *Metal* elements. There may be Metal in the chandelier, but maybe not. Red napkins, blue placemats, a flower arrangement with a patriotic flair of both red and blue flowers, or the use of blue candles in an odd number could help adjust the balance, by bringing in the *Fire* and *Water* elements with color. If the table is staged as if a dinner party is about to begin, the dishes, silverware, candles, and glassware can also help provide the balance.

Make sure the dining room is sparkling clean, smells like cinnamon or French vanilla, and that the lights are on. If you use candles and you have the time, light them . . . but don't go too far. If you have a round rug with the correct colors under the table, you will have extra help in selling your home. The round shape, as you have previously heard, is very positive because it has no "sharp" edges, and the shape introduces some extra *Metal* element. An oval rug would also be slightly more inviting for the guests. A dining room is a staged area. Often it is nothing more than an act, but make sure you carry it off, and you may see a quick sale!

One more thing about lighting, both here and in the rest of the house. Good lighting comes about from understanding the delicate balance between light and shade. Lighting presents space. Light entering surfaces of a room from different angles and heights change their dimensions! It can emphasize height, structure, and materials. It can change focal points and give off different shades of a particular color. With all light can do to a room, good lighting should NOT be noticed. We notice BAD lighting and also how it may draw attention to the wrong elements of a room.

So please just play along and set up the "dream" dining room, create a good balance of the Elements, and whatever you do . . . don't tell anyone this family doesn't really live like this!

Points to Remember

1) This is a stage, and may seem unreal, but please spruce it up
2) Often *Fire* and *Water* are missing here. You don't need a lot, but check carefully and make sure each element is represented.
3) The center piece is a great place to bring in different colors to create the balance that most dining rooms are missing. Candles or flowers can create a focal point that makes the show a winner.
4) Make sure there is a lot of light. Even if your showing is during a sunny day . . . turn on the lights or if willing light the candles. Candles, especially, are very romantic and give off another vibration for the potential buyer.
5) Don't forget, even though it has been proven that most Americans use their dining room infrequently, play it up big time. A well done, staged dining room gives off vibes of family, romance, and success.

Frequently Asked Questions:

My dining room is not in the front of the house, but more in the middle. Is this OK? What do I need to look for?

Actually, a dining room or a kitchen in the middle of your home is great! In our Bagua, the middle gua or area is in Health. Wherever you eat or prepare your food is a good area to have in the Health area. If the dining room is in the Health area, the dominant element is Earth . . . which means colors like earth tones and yellow, shapes that are squares or cubes, and objects made of things like tile, stone, or brick. If you already have these things, you probably have this element covered . . . but make sure! If your floors are wood, the table is glass, and the walls are rose . . . you may be quite void of the primary element of Earth. If you are, you don't really need to get rid of the furniture or paint the walls. You may just need to work on the flower arrangement on the table and place out some yellow place mats. There are many ways to work with what you have.

Our dining area is actually an extension of our great room. There is no wall or divider. What can I do with this set-up?

First place the Bagua over the house and find out where this portion of this room is located. Then set it up to show as an eating area, even if you never use it. It MUST be present! If you don't decide to "play along", the buyers will walk away thinking there is one less room. Cover the table with a tablecloth if 1) the table is old or looks poor; 2) the table has "sharp corners"; or 3) the area needs a missing element. Often a good way to bring in a missing element is to just cover the table with a cheap tablecloth of the right color.

We have no dining room. What can I do?

There must be an eating area in your home. Certainly you have, at least, a breakfast area. You must go through the same steps as above . . . and make it look bigger. Make sure there is no clutter and no extra things in the area. You may want to take a good look at the light fixture again and consider making it better. BUT, get rid of any extra chairs. Get rid of too many plants. Make sure the windows are clean, clean, and clean. Turn the overhead light on during any showing, and play this area up! Full spectrum lighting is very important, and should be the goal when needing help to light a room. Full spectrum lighting eliminates the "spikes" in the color spectrum producing a more balanced white light. This means the colors you see around you are the "true" colors, and not a "washed out" stand-in. With color being so important in Feng Shui, it makes sense that we want the true color of all objects to come out. To understand something better, we say: "shed some light on it". To receive the full understanding and effect we want the real thing . . . the true color showing through.

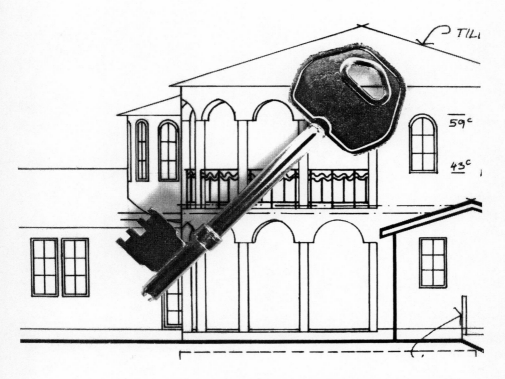

"My precept to all who build is, that the owner should be an ornament to the house, and not the house to the owner."

Cicero

CHAPTER 11

The Living Room and Den

Melinda and Henry knew that a formal living room was not popular with today's home buyers, but after 21 years of marriage, and eight moves all over the country, they had collected quite a few things, with "few" being an understatement. Melinda and Henry were avid antique collectors and a living room was a must as far as they were concerned.

They told their agent that even though they liked the new transitional homes that were being built, they probably needed to concentrate on a traditional home because of their need for extra space . . . primarily a large living room and a comfy den.

First they visited a house that had formal dining and living rooms, at least according to the MLS listing sheet. When they got there it was not apparent to which was which, and they got back in the car not seeing the perfect room for their "stuff".

Later that day, after four other homes, they walked into a home with a huge formal living room up at the front of the house. It was dressed up with some nice older furniture and it had a great conversational area made up in front of the lovely fireplace. It was not cluttered at all and seemed more than big enough for their life time collection. Even though the sellers later confided that they never used the space, it presented exactly the right picture for Melinda and Henry . . . this was their home!

Following up the dining room with the living room is no mistake. Next to the dining room, the living room is the least used room in most homes. Mom seems to want this room to be pristine and only used when the "good company" shows up. Now I don't know about you, but the good company has never been seen this side of the equator in my house! Any way, a living room was once an important room dedicated to the special visitor, or a more intellectual type social gathering, and that seems to have gone the way of the Studebaker. But still, some folks want this type of room to place all of their "good" stuff. And don't make a mistake; we all have a lot of stuff to place somewhere. So, just for this reason, people may want a living room. So, once again we are stuck with making an impression which is not real . . . not quite us!

A formal living room needs to be more Yin than the den, which we will get to in a second. Why more Yin? Because this room is typically used for polite conversation, a quick stopping off place before we are called for dinner, or just a nice place to sit and read. It needs to be "dressed up" in a more Yin fashion so we don't confuse our potential buyer, and as always, we want to appeal to the majority. Too many formal living rooms, in our society, have been turned in to something else. That "something" could be an office, a play room, a craft room, etc. I agree the use of this room has become somewhat murky, but when we are selling . . . don't confuse the buyer! So if the room is set up as a reading room/formal living room, make sure there is task lighting so the buyer does not become confused about the room's purpose.

Again, check out the Bagua for paint colors to consider, but make sure it is "toned" down somewhat. A light grey, a pale yellow, a soft rose are good choices . . . but don't go too dark. A dark blue or green is way too much Yin. Use a healthy dose of accessories in this room, but don't go overboard. If anything, this room needs to be "less" . . . no clutter at all. Make sure there is easy flow and movement through to the next set of rooms. The lighting for a showing should be understated and soft light, with no overheads. Show spaciousness and the opportunity for multiple uses.

Incandescent light is the best type of artificial light because it can be very comforting and welcoming, especially during the evening hours. It can, though, during day time look somewhat unnatural. Incandescent provides full spectrum light compared to **fluorescent** which, even though four times more efficient, gives off a much flatter and less focused light. Never use fluorescent light when showing a home! This type of lighting always gives off a very uncomfortable and unflattering light. *Always* use natural and incandescent light when showing the home. Of course, natural light is always preferred. Open curtains and blinds to let in this full spectrum light. Make sure your windows are cleaned regularly. A thin film of dirt can block up to 50% of your precious sunlight.

The den is a totally different story! This often is the number one gathering place for a family. It has to be more Yang, but also be comfortable at the same time. It goes without saying, that this room needs to be uncluttered, but not "Spartan". Soft leather chairs, large ottomans, some comforters lying out, a roaring fire roaring (in season), blinds open, all the lights turned on, slightly stronger smell (cinnamon?), beautiful music playing, and a few books or magazines strategically left out. The colors you would paint in here could be a little more daring, but again . . . don't go crazy. Brighter colors can have a powerful affect in here, but bringing in Yang accessories with a more modest paint color can do the same trick. Don't forget . . . this room needs to be perceived as a friendly, bonding, active room, where the family gets together often and has a good time. Don't get mixed up with reality, even if your family can't stand each other! We are putting on a performance . . . a play . . . to show our buyers what life could be like if they choose this house.

Use light to highlight unique architecture or a focal point. Wherever light is strongest, that is where the eye goes first. Make sure you lead a visitor's vision to see the best features of a room, and not its worse. If an artificial light directs light upward, your eye and Chi will rise. If it directs light downward, your eye and Chi will sink.

DID YOU KNOW...
The simplest change you can make in the home to combat common depression is to use light...and especially full-spectrum, natural light. Make sure your house never hides its natural light.

In most American homes, the den is located in the back half of the house and will therefore be in either the Marriage corner, the Fame area, or the Wealth corner. For the most part, you will set it up the same way, with some slight changes for each of the different areas. If the den is in the *Marriage/Relationships* area, a pair of doves on a book shelf, a pink pillow, or a photo of you and your significant other would be helpful. But don't go crazy with multiple photos! If the den is located in the *Fame* area, a touch of red, a fireplace, or an award on display will implement the feeling we need. In the *Wealth* corner, a green plant, a purple vase, and old coin collection can boost this area just enough to give off those feelings of success.

Some rooms receive more natural light than others. This can change from season to season. Make sure that if the den receives little natural light during winter, make up for it by adding some artificial, full spectrum light to make the room appear warmer and more comfortable. In some seasons, the "sleepy" Yin can tend to take over and discourage a buyer from getting more interested.

Plants are a VERY good way to enhance the feeling in every room. However, don't go over board and have too many plants; just one or two plants in a room can promote very positive vibrations. Placing a living plant in each room can have a great affect on the atmosphere. Another excellent use of plants is to "soften" sharp corners in any and all rooms. The edges of a fireplace or the corners of a bookcase or table are just a few examples of sharp corners that you will find in a typical home. These edges in Feng Shui cause insecurity for an occupant and can cause a feeling of uneasiness in a visitor. Softening these edges can be another very important way of instilling comfort and compatibility for the potential buyer. A standing plant placed next to a bookcase can soften this sharp corner. Drapes hanging over an area can have this effect. Fabric is often used, as we discussed on a dining room table, to "get rid" of sharp corners.

One more point on lighting: If using a lamp, always take into consideration the lamp shade. The lamp shade CAN greatly change the color of the light and how it affects the colors of the neighboring objects. Always remember, we are staging the place to enable the looker to have a pleasant and comfortable showing . . . a showing that makes them feel like this could be home. We don't want a showing that confuses or shocks; we want a showing that feels welcoming. It could be just the trick to "Sell That House".

Points to Remember:

1) Don't confuse the buyer about the purpose of the room when looking at the living room or den.
2) A living room needs to be more restful and slightly Yin
3) A den needs to convey a more Yang atmosphere, with more emphasis on activity.
4) Keep in mind the location of room with respect to Bagua when choosing colors or accessories
5) Use plants in all rooms if possible, but don't go crazy . . . just a few. This is not the place to put cactus and other spiny plants.
6) Soften as many "sharp corners" as feasible . . . especially ones that may "point" at a visitor when entering each room

Frequently Asked Questions:

My home has neither a formal living room or a den. It has a room called a great room. How should I approach a great room when attempting to sell?
Depending on how big this room is, you may divide the room up somewhat by using partitions or furniture to give off a multiple use feeling. Most great rooms are not much bigger than a den, and need to focus on a more Yang feeling if this is the only, or main, room for people to gather. Think of it as a den, but make sure the flow through your room is easy and not difficult.

I have a living room, but we never use it. It has my mother's couch and chairs that I inherited when she died, and a baby grand piano which has never been played. The wall colors are a sunny yellow and the rug is brown. Should I get rid of everything to show more room and/or paint the walls?

Don't entirely get rid of everything in this room. You may just have too much furniture, resulting in poor traffic flow. Use the chairs and couch to set up a comfy "conversational" area by placing the couch on a wall that has no windows and place the chairs perpendicular to it facing each other. Get rid of the piano so the area is more spacious and less confusing to the buyer for the purpose of the room. The paint color may be a problem. Sunny yellow to me is quite Yang and may not give off a slightly more Yin feeling. You may want to lessen this by checking out the position of this room with respect to the Bagua, find the best colors, and go with a color that is a less vibrant tone.

There's nothing like walking into the wind,
Body bent forward, feeling the force
Knowing raw power,
Tasting its grit
Humbled by the sting of sand
Submitting to a strength
You can't comprehend.

Excerpted from *Nothing Like Wind*
By Raynette Eitel

CHAPTER 12

The Bathrooms

Darren and Karen had known the positive effects of Feng Shui in their old home, and wanted to follow the criteria closely when looking for a new home. Karen had also always wanted a gorgeous master bathroom where she could escape from the world after a stressful day on the job. Karen loved her bath, and wanted to make sure that she and Darren did not compromise on this feature.

They looked at several new home communities, hoping that some of the floor plans would give them what they were looking for, but with no luck. They had always made sure that they took the guidelines of Feng Shui seriously on bathrooms; therefore, the location of the bathrooms were really important to them!

One Saturday, Darren and Karen went to an open house in a neighborhood they had liked. The agent met them at the door, and let them wander around by themselves as he was busy with another couple. It soon became apparent that this home had some real possibilities. The walk up to the front door was curved, the corners inside the house were rounded off, and the landscaping was very appealing . . . but the best thing (at least for Karen), the bathrooms were located away from the front of the house and were quite private. The master bath was located off by itself, was spacious and very inviting. This was a bath that could be worth coming home to!

The half bath downstairs was hidden from view, and was not in the middle of the house under the stairs. Their Feng Shui consultant in Illinois had always made a point of saying to them that this was not a

good location for a bathroom in a house since it was located in the Health
quadrant. Karen was finally feeling like their search was over, and Darren
was glad, too . . . he didn't relish the idea of building from scratch.

The modern bathroom is more than a necessity; in many houses it is a major selling feature. But in Feng Shui, there is really no good place to put a bathroom in a house. If you think about how this idea developed, it made a lot of sense, since early bathrooms and privies were often the source of diseases. But those days are gone. Since we aren't going to eliminate the bathroom from consideration, the best locations, with regard to positioning the bathrooms, is where they are *NOT* . . . . make sure they are NOT in the middle of the house, which is the Health area, or can be seen from the front entrance. These two locations are major mistakes, but there are other secondary situations that should also be addressed. Keep in mind, in Feng Shui, the bathroom is not an area that we want to be the center of attention.

With all bathrooms, regardless if location, keep the doors always shut! Also keep the toilet lids down and the drains closed. This will keep the nourishing Chi swirling around the house, and not allow it to escape easily. Eventually this Chi will leave the house by way of windows, doors, etc., but we never want to give it a quick out through a drain. This will defeat the purpose totally. In Feng Shui, the belief is that your good fortune can literally go *"down the drain"*. Who wants to test that hypothesis? So, what ever you do, and wherever your bathrooms are located, please make sure the doors are shut, the toilet lids are down, and if possible, all drains are closed.

When trying to sell a home, a few additional considerations come into play. A bathroom needs to be outrageously clean! The whole house needs to be cleaner than ever before, but in the bathroom, you need to go even further. There are no shortcuts here. You must roll up your sleeves and make it happen. Deep cleaning is especially important in this area, which means someone needs to get out an old toothbrush and clean the grout, the corners of the room where grime collects, the baseboards, around the faucet, under the sink, the soap dish . . . . you get the idea.

Getting rid of clutter has been discussed in every chapter, but it is especially critical in the bathroom. Many of the items on our bathroom counters are related to personal hygiene, and while the buyers might certainly be pleased the sellers have good hygiene, they really don't want to see the Water-Pik, toothbrush, mouth wash, deodorant and hair care items used every morning. We all experience some sense of discomfort when confronted by other people's personal care items. Since we're creating a fantasy for our potential buyers, someone's toothbrush introduces a jarring note to the picture that just isn't needed. As mentioned with the kitchen, find an accessible storage area for the things used every day, and put the rest away.

We have mentioned smell specifically in Chapter 8, and talked about it in other chapters as well, but I will repeat that information on the bathroom. The bathroom must look and smell absolutely clean. Lemon or citrus odors for a bathroom and kitchen are great, because we associate those smells with cleanliness. We want the buyer to open the door to each and every bathroom, and be very positive about what they see . . . . and smell. Many a bathroom I have shown to a buyer turned them off early in the showing because the owner did not make sure the bathroom(s) were perfect, sanitary, and positive. Don't lose the sale because you ran out of time getting ready one morning, and didn't make the bathrooms fresh and appealing.

It may seem like a simple thing, but the bathroom, especially the master, is your own little place where no one else will bother you. In our society, places like this, where we can get away from the pace and demands for a few minutes are really important to today's buyers. The master bath is a smaller sanctuary inside the overall sanctuary of the home. As you probably will acknowledge, people are putting more and more money into a special bathroom environment. Most builders know this is a strong trend for people looking at new construction. They are making sure their bathrooms knock the socks off potential buyers. Why . . . because a glamorous bathroom is in demand by consumers!

What is the number one room that homeowners upgrade? The kitchen is first, and the master bath is a strong second. So, take advantage of this information, and make sure your client's bathrooms, especially the master, show the best that they can. Aim for the "*spa*" environment so important to today's consumer. Place fresh, colorful towels, a plant or two, candles, and/or fresh flowers in the area. Bamboo is great choice for the bathroom . . . it flourishes in low light, high humidity conditions, is easy to care for, and is also considered to be "lucky". A spotless shower curtain, squeaky clean shower doors, and a great smelling, spotless toilet bowl, tub and sink will go along way towards keeping the buyers happy while touring your home. Ensure the area is well lighted; this may be an area where the seller wants to spend a few dollars to upgrade the fixtures.

DID YOU KNOW...
In Feng Shui, there is really NO good place for a bathroom, but there are some places worse than others. If possible, never have a bathroom in the middle of your downstairs.

If the bathroom is missing one or more of the Five Elements, consider bringing in or changing the throw rug, changing the color of the towels, or adding a candle or two in the color needed to create balance. Bathrooms usually have plenty of the *Water* element, but the other elements may be less obvious. The element most likely to be missing in the bathroom is *Fire;* a few strategically placed candles can address that while contributing to the idea of relaxing in a pleasant bath.

Once again, there is no good place for this necessary modern invention . . . so we must work around it, glamorize it as much as possible, and keep the darn door shut!

Points to Remember:

1) Clean, clean, and then clean some more.
2) If you change the smell from the rest of the house, consider lemon
3) Keep doors shut always.
4) Always keep the toilet lid down.
5) Close the drain.
6) Accessories like towels, rugs, soaps, candles, and plants can give the balance needed for The Five Elements. It is always easy to pick up the right colors in a bathroom by using accessories, so don't repaint unless the color is too Yang. A red or orange bathroom may look good to you, but it will only keep the buyers looking at another home.

Frequently Asked Questions:

If my bathroom is red, is this a problem?
Quite possibly it will be for a perspective home buyer. Don't forget, when attempting to sell a home, the colors you gravitate towards are not always the best ones to sell with. A bathroom is primarily a Yin setting. Red and bright yellow are more aggressive and do not lend themselves to an opportunity for you to be alone and maybe think. Don't create any bathroom setting for a buyer which gives off a feeling of having to rush.

One of my bathrooms is located in the middle of the downstairs. Is this a big problem, or can I assume they will not care?
A bathroom in the Health area of a home will be disconcerting for most people. It is disturbing the energy pattern and it really has no good way to release energy. Closing the doors will help. Keeping the toilet seat and lid down will help. But make a special effort to ensure that the aromas coming from here are very positive and slightly more sweet (smelling). Hanging a crystal inside the door or in the middle of the room, if it is a large bathroom, will help disperse energy more evenly also.

© Photographer: Rashid Iqbal | Agency: Dreamstime.com

Water in its many forms soothes the jangled nerves,
Isn't this a pleasure that everyone deserves?

Excerpted from *Water*
By Adelaide Rhead

CHAPTER 13

The Master Bedroom

Myra had been living in a suburb of Boston in the same house for almost 34 years. Ever since Sam, her husband of 45 years, had died she had been thinking of moving to a more manageable place. This place was just too big, and all the kids thought it was time to consider an apartment or even a condo.

Myra decided to take their advice, so she hired a local Realtor who had helped her daughter Pam and son-in-law Jeff sell their home and find their current home in Dorchester. They felt that Ken would do a good job for her, and could help her decide where to move to. Ken told Myra that her home was very spacious for the area, since it had 4 bedrooms, but that it needed some updating. Myra and Sam had made very few changes down through the years and now it showed. Ken especially wanted Myra to strongly consider changing out the carpet, updating the kitchen lighting and counter tops, and moving her master bedroom into the 21st Century!

Myra didn't think these changes were necessary; she told Ken that the home was well maintained and that a buyer would change it to match their tastes. Ken enlisted Pam's help about the kitchen, and Myra gave in and spent the money to make it more modern. But she drew the line about changing her bedroom; it was perfectly fine, it suited her, and she and Sam had picked out these colors together years ago!

Ken placed Myra's home on the market, and initially there was a lot of traffic, but as the weeks went by, fewer and fewer appointments were made. After three months, Myra was getting tired of the process of having strangers go through her house, keeping it clean, and leaving the home when someone came for a showing. Ken shared the feedback and it had been universally consistent . . . the house shows dark, shows old, and looks like it needs work.

Pam and Jeff sat down one day and talked with Ken about why Myra's home hadn't even got an offer. Ken told them about the comments and how the home needed to show more modern in the eyes of the buyers. Many of their comments had addressed the gloomy, dark look of the master suite. They left the house feelings somewhat down . . . not positive! Ken told them that the three rooms that would have the biggest impact were the kitchen, the main living area, and the master bedroom.

So, with Pam and Jeff's help, Ken was able to persuade Myra to change the master bedroom, the entrance to the house, which was dark, and the carpet. The bedroom was in the Marriage corner when situating the Bagua, which was good, but the room was a dark blue and the carpet was a dingy brown. The entire house had wall to wall carpet, with different colors in each room, and needed to be changed as it was over 20 years old.

The family picked out, with Ken's help, a lighter color beige carpet that was placed throughout the house, they re-painted the master bedroom a lovely rose, got rid of the colorless comforter and placed a new one of white in its place, changed the wattage of lights throughout the house to give off more light, and made sure the entrance was transformed by placing pots of yellow plants next to the front door.

Within days, there were a couple of showings that went very well. One of them actually came back a second time, and let Ken know it was at the top of their list. Another couple came out two days later, and before the other couple could make up their minds, made an offer that was easy to negotiate. Myra was finally on her way to a new life without having to mow the lawn again!

I'm sure if you have been in this wacky business long enough, you'd agree how important the master bedroom and its bath are to a successful sale of a home. If the master bedroom is not big enough or not situated in the right corner of the house or if the walk-in closet is too small or the light is not good enough or the room has wall paper . . . well, you've heard it all, just like I have!! The master suite can be more than enough to derail an offer from a perspective buyer. Your customer wants a nice retreat from the world out side . . . maybe more than ever.

Stress seems to be a key word we hear everywhere. There is stress driving to work, and our commutes have gotten longer and longer. There is stress at work trying to keep the boss, the clients, and the fellow workers pleased. There is stress trying to get to the mall or the grocery store. Everyone wants a place to retire to that buffers them from these factors . . . at least until the next day.

More and more builders are creating these lovely, large, high-ceiling, getaways for us to enjoy. Lets face it, even when we get home . . . we sometimes even need to get away from the kids! A luxurious master bedroom can be that little slice of heaven . . . . a place where we can relax, rejuvenate, read a good book, or rest when we are feeling poorly. Everyone needs a place that they can call their own.

Using the Bagua as our guide, the perfect place to have this "retreat" would be in the far right back corner when facing the house. As you know, this is the Relationship or Marriage corner. Even if the room is not located in this area, advise your sellers to make this room a treat for themselves, as well as for the potential buyers. In Feng Shui, the bedroom is to be used for just two things, and nothing else. Those two things are romance and restoration. So begin by getting rid of televisions, computers, and work-related items in here. These items tend to be confusing to a buyer . . . is this a bedroom . . . or is it an office? More importantly, these items interfere with relationships. This is a good idea for the sellers to follow even when they move into their next home.

After clearing out the electronic equipment, furniture placement should be the next consideration. Feng Shui has many special rules about bed placement and appropriate color choice in a bedroom to make sure that the individuals achieve total restoration for the next day. The logic is if you don't get perfect rest, you will begin the day fatigued, and that will cause you to fall down on your other pursuits. For instance, if you have a poor night's sleep, you may be cranky the next morning and pick a fight with your spouse or your boss.

In other words, bad sleep equals bad temper equals quarrel which eventually could equal divorce or unemployment. Of course, sleepless nights will also affect the most important thing in Feng Shui . . . your health! If your health goes, so does your relationships, your success, and your dreams! So our focus is on an environment that gives us a perfect night's sleep, and hopefully, advances our relationships in positive ways.

In Feng Shui, there are perfect places to place the bed. The drawing provides the best location to put your bed, starting with #1 as the best, #2 the next best, and so forth. Moving the bed into a good Feng Shui position will create a subconscious sense of balance and harmony with a perspective buyer. Suggest your clients consider moving their bed if it is in an especially bad position. When a person sleeps with feet pointing straight out the door #5, it is considered poor. This is called the "coffin" position, for obvious reasons, and permits the entering Chi to be more forceful then desirable.

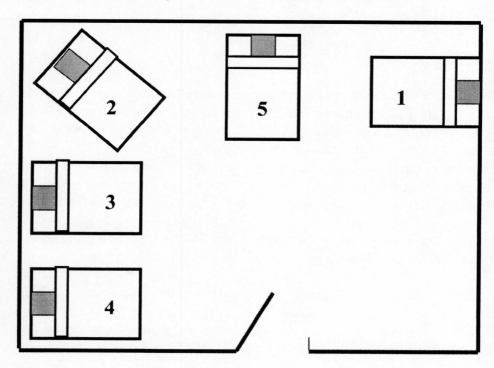

Please make sure the bedroom is VERY Yin. Many of today's bedrooms are often quite Yang. Think about the vibrant colors and decorations many teenagers prefer, and you'll begin to get the sense of what I mean. Maybe the teenager is sleeping fine with this combination, but it is also possible that those red walls are interfering with a perfect night's sleep! The best colors for a bedroom are darker shades of green, blue, or brown, although it is important to watch the impact of these colors. We don't want the room too dark. For example, dark blue can be depressing for some folks. Colors associated with all skin tones work well as does some shades of pink. The room should be painted a color that does not create unusual energy or excitement, but you want to avoid white in any bedroom, as it is too neutral and sterile. The Yang colors, like yellow, are great for an office where attention and energy are called for, but not a bedroom, where rest and relaxation are the goals.

Again, if your owners say "the buyers can just go out after buying the home and re-paint", please make them understand that a home or a room that is confusing with respect to use will keep their home on the market much longer. If the bedroom that needs to be repainted is the teenager's room, get the child on board by explaining that this is a temporary situation and they must help the family get the house sold. It is my opinion that most kid's rooms, especially teenagers, will have to have the rooms re-painted. That purple room is not going to cut it with that little old lady from Pasadena. Black might look good on your daughter, but she must understand that a black room is a HUGE turnoff and VERY confusing to anyone looking at it. I know . . . how about that cute little girl's bedroom that is painted hot pink? PAINT IT!! Don't confuse the buyers, and don't give them the idea that the first thing they will need to do when they buy this house is to paint the rooms. A buyer is not interested in having to work when they move in. Yes, the mural that took the seller two months to paint is quite lovely, but the buyers only see the work they need to put into repainting it. Before they put an offer on your listing, they will first try to find a house that has no work to be done.

DID YOU KNOW...
Scientists have proven that the color blue will slow down a person's breathing and pulse rates.

Bedrooms are a touchy subject. They are very personal, and certainly show the unique tastes of the sellers, but selling a home is not the time to have a contest for originality. No, our goal is to get the home sold as quickly as possible. Often a bedroom is out of balance not only with Yin and Yang, but often with respect to The Five Elements. Most bedrooms are missing one or more of the elements. Make it a priority to walk through each bedroom with the information from *Chapter 6: The Five Elements*, checking off items which give each and every element. This is especially important in the master bedroom. The master must be perfect, or as close as possible, so refer to the chart often when trying to achieve this balance. The room has to feel right to a stranger coming in for the first time. Is it missing a touch of *Fire*? One red pillow on the bed may make a big difference. Is there too much *Earth* in this room? We can just counteract it by using the "Destructive Cycle" we discussed in Chapter 6.

Make a thorough inventory of all of the elements and test it with a neighbor or your significant other. Move some things and try again. The master suite will make or break you, so try to get it as right as possible. And as in all other rooms, don't forget the *Five Senses*. The bedroom should take on the aroma that you have decided to use throughout the house. Make sure it is subtle. When considering the visual sense, don't ignore lighting. Normal ceiling fixtures can create harsh, artificial patterns of light and shadow, rarely flattering to the room or the people in it. **Uplighting** enhances a sense of height, making a room appear more spacious than it is. This is an excellent way to lighten corners, make ceilings look higher, and to give more flexibility to your efforts. Uplighting can be moved from corner to corner or room to room. The principal purpose of uplights is to direct light up at the ceiling . . . which then reflects it back. Uplights improve the Yang of a dark room by being uplifting without being overpowering.

With respect to the other bedrooms, make them un-cluttered, clean, and spacious as possible. Staging these rooms is NOT as important as making a lasting impression in the master bedroom. Just reducing clutter may be all that is needed in these rooms. Consider getting rid of 30 to 50% of the things in all of these bedrooms . . . and that includes the *closet!* Little things, like extra room in the closet, will put this house on top of the buyers' list.

Points to Remember:

1) The master IS one of the most important rooms with respect to a buyer making a decision.
2) Consider re-painting a child's room. It is not costly and will make a big impression. A wildly colored room will also make an impression . . . the wrong one!
3) Pay special attention to the Yin/Yang of all bedrooms.
4) Pay special attention to The Five Elements in the master.
5) Did I already say this . . . pay special attention to the master?

Frequently Asked Questions

Are you saying that the other bedrooms are not that important to a quick sale, and if so, why worry about them?
The master suite is more important, and MUST be its best . . . but you can still lose a sale if not paying attention on the other bedrooms. Remember this one thing: a buyer does NOT want to move in and work on the house. You must make sure these rooms are not "wild". You must make sure these rooms show "large". You must make sure the other bedrooms show "un-cluttered".

My master bedroom is NOT in the Relationship area of the house. Is this going to hurt me when I sell?
No, not really! In the room that is in the relationship area, add a small touch that represents relationships to make sure a visitor does not feel anything is missing. For example, just add a pair of pink flowers or two playful figurines, or add a picture of you and your significant other. Then follow the same rules as outlined in the chapter to stage your master bedroom to show its best!

What makes the cool and gentle breeze? "Tis Wind;
What makes the boughs and leaves to dance? "Tis Wind
What makes the autumn leaves to fall? "Tis Wind;
What makes the honey bees to fly? "Tis Wind;

Excerpted from *The Wind*
By John Celes

CHAPTER 14

The Outside and the Entrance

John and Lynn had moved to Belmont several months ago, and wanted to get to know the area a little before getting serious about finding a home. They religiously checked the classifieds and the small real estate magazines with the color pictures to find a home that might fit their needs.

All most every weekend, John and Lynn called on homes that looked good in the magazine or read well in the paper. Often they would ride out to three or four homes on a Saturday to improve their knowledge of the area and perhaps locate a home worth looking at. Often their first impression was poor. Sometimes they felt the ads or pictures were not exactly accurate in their description.

They decided one week to contact a real estate agent they had previously talked with, and made an appointment with her to visit several homes. Their criteria were fairly well defined, but they wanted the home to be unique; not just one of those "cookie cutter" homes they often ran across in developments. Jena, their agent, made appointments for five homes that seemed to meet their needs and their pocket book, and picked them up at their apartment. The first home mentioned being close to amenities and having great curb appeal. When they pulled in front of it, they felt like the homeowner's definition of curb appeal and theirs were at opposite ends of the spectrum. They went in, and were somewhat disappointed with the floor plan, but were especially uncomfortable with the way it looked outside.

Jena took them by the other four homes, but they became more and more disenchanted with the way the homes looked. They flatly declined to

*even visit the last one. John and Lynn didn't care as much about an extra
100 to 200 square feet as they did about the appearance of the home . . .
they wanted a home that inspired them when they pulled up.*

How the outside of a home looks may determine more than anything else whether a home sells quickly. If you think that just working on the inside will be enough, you will be sadly mistaken. An attractive, magnetizing outside will improve your buyer traffic greatly. Curb appeal has always been known to be important, but we often think a mowed lawn, weeded beds, no cars parked in the drive, and a hidden trash can is enough. Well it isn't, especially if you want to sell a home quickly and for top dollar.

This chapter will help you to improve the curb appeal of your listings. You want to be just as interested in "attracting" buyers by using Feng Shui to subconsciously allure them to make an appointment, as you are in the physical changes you may need to make in the process. You may have trouble believing that some small changes can actually entice a person to call you off your sign . . . but I don't . . . I've seen it work. Laying the Bagua over the entire lot gives us particular areas we MUST enhance to achieve our goal.

Just as we identified each "Gua" or area of the Bagua inside the house, we can do the same with the entire lot. The front right area is the *Helpful People* area, and as I said in the house . . . this area is quite important. It needs to be VERY attractive and well groomed. This area alone will be like a giant magnet. Here is what want you to do in this area:

- Move the real estate sign to the *helpful people* area. We want potential buyers to notice the house AND the listing agent's name and phone number.

- move the flyer box to the helpful people area, also . . . and if possible, use either brightly colored paper, or use white paper with colored photos.

- around the sign, either plant some yellow flowers or place three pots of yellow flowers around it.

- if possible, place a gazing ball or something spherical in the bed next to the house in this quadrant.

- make sure that the whole lot is mowed well, kept watered, and edged.

- a big help would be to plant multi-colored flowers in a bed to the right front of house.

Going to the left, in the middle of the house, we have the *Career* area. This area is also a MUST to improve. If you have a path to the front door, make sure it is NOT a straight shot to the entrance. We would like the sidewalk or path to meander or curve. A straight path will permit our Chi to forcibly head quickly with much force to our front door and then through the house. We must break this up by causing the walk to look like it is curving. If it is straight, place an odd number of potted plants on opposite sides in a staggered pattern. One is on the right, and then one is on the left, then one on the right, and so on. This again creates a sort of curving path as these plants become obstacles which the Chi coming off the street must move around, therefore slowing it down considerably.

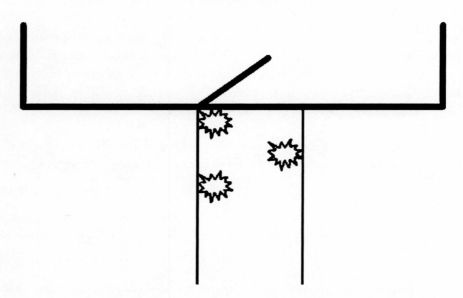

After making sure the path or walk is fine, we need to check the entrance to the front door. If we have the potential buyers interested up to this point, we can lose them here. A sorry entrance will scare many a buyer. This is a critical first impression. This area is in the Career area and *Water* is the dominant element. The front door must give a good impression. As we stated earlier, the front door is called the *"Mouth of Chi"*, because this is where energy enters the home. In the Orient, a red door is especially powerful, but is less common in western countries. You may be hesitant to use red, but dark blue or black (Water!) is great, and dark shades of green or brown are fine. Make sure the hardware (kick plate, door knocker, door knob, house numbers, and lanterns) is polished to a bright shine, or maybe even consider replacing it if it can't be nicely polished. New hardware will give off amazing vibrations to a visitor . . . it shouts "Welcome". Nothing will get them more excited about looking inside than a gorgeous entrance.

Place black pots on both sides of front door with either red or yellow flowers in them. Check out the welcome mat; in many homes it is dirty, worn and tired. Replace it with a brand new black one. If it is a semi-circle shape, it will be even more auspicious . . . since this shape and color represents the *Water* element.

Moving clockwise to the left front of the house and lot is the *Knowledge* area. Planting some flowers that are blue or adding some green plants here will be very positive. The next area on the left side of the house is the *Family* area, and we will not do anything big here. Just make sure this area is well maintained. Do not make the mistake of putting the garbage cans here or anywhere outside. Stow the cans inside the garage if at all possible; regardless make sure they are out of sight.

The back left corner is the *Wealth* area and should be, of course, well maintained, but also add a touch of purple here with flowers or gazing balls. If you have a tree or trees in this area, it is very positive. If you do not, consider adding a small tree to represent growing wealth and success for an occupant.

The next area, *Fame*, is REALLY important and needs to have special attention paid to it. Make sure this area does not have too much of the Water element. If it does, add some Earth to damp the effect and up the Fire even more! Red flowers need to be present in this area on a patio or deck and in the back of the property also. Adding three pots of red flowers on a patio (or deck) that can be seen from inside will give off great benefits and add greatly to selling a house. Please use odd numbers and evenly space them.

The far right corner is the *Relationship or Marriage* corner and it can be a powerful attractor for buyers if you have a neighborhood that caters to couples. Pink is the color I would like added here.

DID YOU KNOW...
When the main door, *The Mouth of Chi*, has nothing that threatens it from inside or out, the Chi that enters is powerful and brings good fortune.

The right side of the house is located in *Children and Creativity* and does not need anything special done to it. Just make sure it is well taken care of and has no clutter.

The outside of the house is initially more important than the inside and **MUST** be perfected to allow us to meet our goal. If the curb appeal is lacking, you'll have trouble getting the potential buyers inside . . . and if they don't come in, it doesn't matter what it looks like. If your budget is not much, use it to bring in flowers and color in the appropriate places and you will see the results!

Major Points to Remember:

1) The outside is initially more important than the inside. If you only have so much to invest in getting your home ready to sell, do it here!
2) The three most important areas to enhance are: Career, Helpful People, and Fame.
3) Use the Bagua to help you use the right colors.
4) The front door will make you or break you.

Frequently Asked Questions:

Looking at the Bagua, do I have to use the primary colors associated with these areas?
These are the best, but you could easily substitute the colors that are on both sides. For example: the primary color in the Wealth area is purple. On the right is red and on the left is green. These colors can also be used nicely.

Shouldn't I enhance ALL areas and not just the three you mentioned above?
NO! Always enhance these three—Career, Helpful People, and Fame—and maybe pick a fourth to emphasize a neighborhood quality (like the children/creativity area if this neighborhood is very child-focused), but don't enhance all. The reason not to do everything is that too much activity will subtract from the emphasis on the important areas.

Is the entrance really THAT important?
Boy is it ever!!! If you fail here, you can forget a quick sale. If you fail here, you will get "low ball" offers. Pay special attention to this area . . . please! Think of your house as having to pass specific tests. The first test a house must pass to be considered by a potential buyer is the "drive up" test or curb appeal. If the house doesn't *WOW* them when they drive up, you have a major obstacle to get their interest. The second "test" is at the front door. The third "test" is in the foyer, and so forth. You must have a house that keeps passing the "tests", and if the front door doesn't pass, the buyers may never get inside!

Mid pleasures and palaces though we may roam
Be it ever so humble, there's no place like home.

John Howard Payne
(1791-1852)

CHAPTER 15

Feng Shui Savvy Customers

The Walkers were from New York City, and had a lot of powerful experiences with the philosophy of Feng Shui, used throughout the city. Moving to Tennessee was exciting because they'd be closer to their grandchildren, but they knew they wanted to make sure their new home would be Feng Shui compatible with their pursuits. They wanted to be able to work with a real estate agent who could be sensitive to their wishes, and hopefully versed in this philosophy.

They knew that certain lots were missing parts of life functions, and wanted to ensure themselves a positive existence in their new life in Tennessee. Other items in the house would also be a big problem to overcome, and they really didn't want to use up their energy to try to cure these problems either.

Their daughter-in-law found them an agent who had worked with several customers who needed this kind of help, and she turned out to be exactly what they needed to make this transition a good one for them. As with their last home, the Walkers found out that a house with raised "Chi" automatically raised the value, even if the sellers weren't aware of the principles of Feng Shui. They wanted to make a sound real estate investment, one that appreciated nicely.

As I've alluded to . . . many more potential home buyers in the United States are taking Feng Shui seriously, and WILL keep particular things in mind when looking for that special home. As a real estate agent, it would be smart if you knew the major things that turn off a Feng Shui savvy buyer.

Not only will a buyer from China, Taiwan, Japan, Thailand, Malaysia, India, or Tibet be so inclined, but know that these days you will have serious Feng Shui buyers from Europe and other parts of the United States. In some states, like California, Florida, and New York, your real estate employer very possibly will ask you to have some experience with these ideas.

To begin with, a home that has a more regular shape . . . a square, rectangle, circle, octagon . . . would be easier for a Feng Shui savvy buyer to consider. Of course, some of these shapes will probably NOT be found in your MLS search, but they may well bring this up. Most newer homes, built in the late 1990s until the present, are not a "regular" shape. A lot of the homes we see are more "U" shaped or "L" shaped, or some variation on this shape. Of course, a normal two-story home is easy, but it, as you will see, has its own set of Feng Shui problems. High, two-story foyers or great rooms give concerns also, but can be addressed.

The perfect ideal home for an admirer of Feng Shui would probably be a home that is a rectangle, but we probably will have to contend with something else. In all cases, if the home is not a perfect shape . . . we want to be able to "square" it off . . . and create the allusion of it being an acceptable shape.

The location of the lot is VERY important. When showing homes to someone who wants to take this philosophy strongly into account, the lot shape and location can quickly sink any consideration. If you have the opportunity, I would preview homes before you show them to save you time . . . and aggravation. At least, do a drive by and check out the lots.

DID YOU KNOW...
Feng Shui is used all over the world. Even if the potential buyers entering your home are not versed in this philosophy, often they will feel uneasy on a sub-conscious level if some things are poorly placed.

For instance, any home that is at a dead-end will probably not be considered. This situation gives no outlet for the Chi when it comes down a street. It becomes frustrated and confused, and is not the best for attracting and using this energy. A cul-de-sac is NOT much better! The lot will automatically NOT be a square or rectangle, but more of a pie shape . . . so we have a squaring problem. Also, energy tends to come into a cul-de-sac and swirl around and be uneven. Confusion sets in here also.

One of the worst places, in Feng Shui thinking, to set a house is in a T-Junction. A T-Junction is where one street runs right at your house and another is also parallel to it . . . therefore creating a "T". This type of set up has lots of rushing Chi coming off the roads, before even considering traffic and their headlights. A junction like this is not as secure, not as quiet, and not as private . . . as would be desired. The cures for these situations are similar. Landscaping to block some of the rushing energy off the roads would be beneficial.

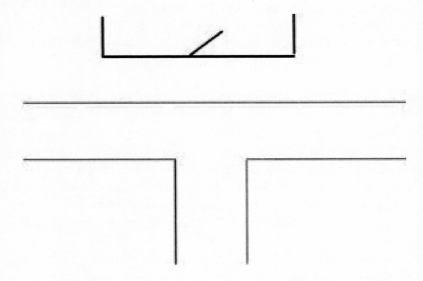

The perfect setting for a home would be on a flat lot or one in which the house sits up slightly. Having a house up really high is never a good situation for anyone. In Feng Shui, this creates too much effort or loss of energy for an individual to drive or walk up to their home. BUT even worse, is when a home sits below grade! A house that sits down below the street is seen as having Chi move over top or missing the house. There are cures, but most buyers will not be interested in looking at a home like this.

The neighbors and their homes need to be looked at closely also. If the house you are considering showing is smaller or lower than the ones on either side, you may have sharp corners facing the house giving off "poison arrows", and you also may have negative feelings like inferiority. It is always best if the homes you are showing have roof lines that are basically on the same plane, or the home you are showing is somewhat higher. Don't bother showing a home that is "dwarfed" by the homes adjacent to it.

I've already mentioned irregular lots. The perfect lot would be very close to a square or rectangle shape. When a lot is pie shape or very strangely configured, a person may feel not totally complete. A lot can be "cured" by squaring it, but make sure they are OK with this possibility, or you may be, once again, wasting your time and theirs.

If a home sits way too far back on a lot, the buyer may not like this either! The best place for a home to sit on a lot is somewhat closer to the front boundary. A home sitting on the front third, or at least the front half, is best for Feng Shui purposes.

A different situation to take into account is the buyer's view. It is certainly always preferred to have a beautiful view when you look out your front door, but lets face it . . . in today's building atmosphere of subdivisions, often the homeowners are lucky if their view is just another home. Views or proximity to a cemetery, funeral home, police station, hospital, or a sewage treatment plant will not be even considered. The Feng Shui savvy buyer considers these views very inauspicious and do want to see these places or even be close to them. For that matter, buyers who aren't Feng Shui savvy will probably object, as well.

Certain types of homes like split-levels and tri-levels are not positive. The thinking here is that the Chi enters the home, gets confused about which direction to take, and ends up not doing a good job. Any home with lots of levels and stairs may be a poor choice for you Feng Shui buyer.

Water on a property can be positive, but not always. There are certain locations where it can be pleasing, but if the property has water in the back or running through it . . . the buyer may have reservations. Water in the front should not be really close to the house and hopefully not have movement away from the structure.

Sidewalks, paths, and driveways should also be scrutinized greatly. A direct (straight) path to the front door is NOT good. The idea is that the Chi is not slowed down sufficiently and is very forceful coming through the front door, which again is the **Mouth of Chi**. A winding or curved pathway is very positive!

If power lines, which already are considered an eyesore in the U.S., cross a lot or the house, the buyers look poorly at this situation because of the electrical discharge given off. Anything that has the potential to have an adverse effect on a person's physical or mental health is to be avoided.

The **front door** has a lot of symbolism in this ancient art, but it is also a quick way for a person to check out some problems. In homes currently being built, the *WOW* factor is the norm. For example, many two-story homes now have two-story foyers or two-story great rooms. Too often when people walk into one of these homes, they can actually see right out to the backyard. The visual path is exactly what energy will do when it enters your house . . . it will go straight back outside without nourishing the home. We want a home to have the entering Chi to stay awhile and circulate. We want it to be slow and thorough, not fast and gone! So, a house that has this dramatic flair may not be to your Feng Shui buyers' taste, unless the foyer area is "cured" by creating an impediment to force a detour. This detour forces a different path for the Chi. It makes it meander instead of rush through the environment.

Another thing that is a problem at the front is when the front door directly faces a stairway. A positioning like this easily allows energy to flow up and down the stairway without considering the room on the right or to the left. Since we are all about having the energy circulate and nourish the whole house, this REALLY defeats the purpose. So when checking out a two story or a one and half story, stairways in the back or to the side are best.

As mentioned, drains are a continual source of worry in Feng Shui. An open drain is an invitation for Chi to go right down, and leave the house quickly. Positions of kitchens and particularly bathrooms are crucial to the decision of a Feng Shui savvy buyer. If you can see a bathroom or kitchen from the front door, this is poor. This type of buyer would rather the kitchen is in the back of the house, and that a bathroom on the first floor is NOT in the middle of the house (Health area). The kitchen can be in the middle of a house, but the buyer would still prefer not being able to see it when entering through the front door. As earlier stressed, keep all doors to bathrooms closed, all drains shut, and toilet lids down.

Some homes have beams in the ceilings, and can be OK if painted a neutral color so they blend in, but always think of "duration" and "proximity". If located in a study and a person uses this room sporadically . . . no problem. But if they work in a room with beams day after day; and hour after hour, we have a problem. So of course the worst place to have exposed beams is the bedroom, and especially the master bedroom. If there are beams in these rooms, probably they will want to keep on looking.

Some homes, especially older homes, have long dark hallways. Hallways like this are not conductive to a good flow of Chi. It would be better, if this was not the case . . . but they are easily cured by placing some colorful artwork along the walls, and putting up a mirror and the end of the hall. Today, newer homes have a different way of spreading out the rooms, and often you won't find this problem. But, if your market is an older home, you may run across this and will need to field the complaint.

Feng Shui always has as a bottom line, the idea of security. We do our best work in a safe environment. We certainly find it easier carrying on a conversation if we feel secure doing it. The following are room positions that would cause the inhabitant anxiety and therefore not allow for the kind of existence to reach your goals:

1) If a bedroom is situated over a garage; the idea being there is no stability for the one who sleeps here;

2) a bedroom is over top a bathroom or utility room . . . bathrooms continue to get a bad rap in Feng Shui;

3) The wall in a bedroom where the bed is likely to go backs up to a wall that has a bathroom or some type of plumbing on the other side. Any problems with plumbing or wiring in the walls give off bad vibes. Again, we think of an environment as corresponding to a human body. So, this would represent an internal problem (blood vessels).

Some buyers you run in to may want their home to face a particular direction, and insist on it. Long ago, a home facing south was considered very auspicious, but you will also find a buyer who, depending on their birth date, may have four positive directions and four negative directions they want to consider. All I can tell you is, if you want their business . . . get a good compass!

Points to Remember:

1. Check out the position of the house on the lot.
2. Try to show a lot that is regular
3. Check the grade . . . make sure the house is not below grade.
4. Really irregular lots are probably a waste of time.
5. Make sure the home is not next to something negative, like a cemetery.
6. Be careful of water on the property and where it is situated.
7. No split levels!

8. Straight walks are not positive . . . look for curves.
9. No power lines.
10. No direct view of backyard from front door.
11. No stairway facing the front door.
12. Watch out for exposed beams, especially in master bedroom.
13. Forget long dark halls.
14. No bedroom over a garage or a bathroom.
15. Headboard of bed can not be on a wall that shares drains.
16. No toilets in the center of house.
17. Plumbing and wiring are in good shape or new.
18. The soil supports lush vegetation and encourages wild life.
19. The house is situated in a perfect "armchair" setting.
20. The houses on either side are not significantly larger.
21. The lot has mostly hardwood trees and little if any pine trees.
22. The house is not situated on a T-junction.
23. The house is not on a dead-end.
24. The house is not on a corner lot.
25. The house is not directly at the end of a cul-de-sac.
26. The house is not totally sharp, all 90 degree corners.
27. The kitchen is located so as not viewed from the front door.
28. No bathroom is located in the center of the house.
29. The master suite, if on the first floor, was situated in the back, and hopefully in the far right corner.
30. The master bedroom is separated from a bathroom by a door.
31. The house has plenty of sunlight.
32. A bathroom is not visible from the front door.
33. The front door does not have a blocked view, like a tree or a wall.

The following are cures for each problem, if you are listing a home with these problems, and want to appeal to the Feng Shui buyer.

1. If the lot is irregular, try to square it off using a plant, flag, or artwork.
2. A regular lot, which is good, is a square, rectangle, or circle.
3. If the lot is below grade, situate a light or two outside that shines upwards on to the roof.
4. If you can't figure out how to square the lot in some way, forget it.
5. If the house is next to a funeral home, fire hall, cemetery, etc. secure a Bagua mirror and place it outside and point it towards the problem.

6. A pool in the backyard or a lake may be too much of a good thing. Consider the elements and add some Earth and plants that minimize the effect.

7. You may be able to use mirrors or crystals to manipulate the energy in the area.

8. Stagger plants along the walkway to create a meandering or curved path

9. If there are power lines, use a Bagua mirror

10. Place an obstacle in the way of this direct path . . . like a plant, water fountain, and artwork. A crystal also may distribute the energy to other rooms

11. This allows energy or Chi to move in and out without pausing. A plant at the bottom of the stairway will force the energy to detour . . . a crystal at the bottom of the steps may do the trick also.

12. Paint the beams a neutral color and try to get them to blend in

13. A mirror at the end of the hallway will allow more natural light to be present. Artwork on the walls on both sides will also help.

14. There is no good way to give the resident of this bedroom a feeling of stability. Move them!

15. Move the bed

16. Hang a crystal in on the bathroom inside door to disperse energy, keep doors shut at all times, always keep toilet lid down, and close all drains.

17. Make sure these items are inspected and made right.

18. Bad soil means less wildlife activity and an absence of good Chi. Add good topsoil or go to the next house.

19. A house with a hill or mountain behind for support and protection of some sort on both sides, like trees, and a wide view up front is perfect.

20. When homes on either side are dominant it gives a lack of confidence . . . try to keep looking

21. If the lot has a lot of pines, look to replace them over time with hardwoods

22. You are getting rushing Chi from two situations . . . too much of a good thing. Put up a barrier, wall, or some type of reflective surface.

23. If the house is at the end of a dead-end street, the Chi has no place to go . . . you will need to work very hard on getting its attention by

manipulating the energy to come towards your house. Mirrors, gazing balls, etc.

24. Read #22
25. You need a barrier to slow it down and then re-direct it at a slower pace to the front door,
26. You need to soften corners by using fabric (like drapes) or plants. Try not to sit with your back to a sharp corner.
27. If the kitchen is visible from the front door, try to block view by closing a door, putting up a screen, or using a buffer of sorts (furniture, etc.)
28. If there is a bathroom in the center, close the door and hang a crystal inside the room behind the door.
29. Make sure your room is behind the mid-point of the house and behind any children's room, or they may feel they are in command.
30. Keep the door shut at all times
31. Pull blinds up and curtains off or wide open
32. Same as 27
33. Cut trees down, move wall, or place mirrors in such a way to be able to see around the obstacle.

Less is More

Robert Browning
(1812-1889)

CHAPTER 16

Feng Shui and the Open House

For many many years, every real estate agent has used the staple in real estate—the standard *Open House*. Despite the expectation that this will be part of the selling experience, the Open House is often maligned by everyone, including the homeowner and the agent. After a boring three hours sitting on the couch at an Open House where no one shows up, an agent is usually not in any hurry to get back into the "saddle".

Not only are Open Houses traditionally "done", they even have traditional times. Typically, they are done on the weekend,; the reasoning being that attendance will be better when people have more free time. Sundays have often been used, but Saturdays are a close second. Afternoons are usually preferred over the mornings, but there is no reason to dismiss a late morning Open House on a Saturday.

Normally, the procedure for conducting an Open House begins with the placement of a yard sign on a Wednesday or Thursday, announcing the date and time of the Open House. This gives passers-by a chance to record in their minds about the upcoming event. Often a subdivision (or town) will have regulations about when you can place signs, but if you can . . . don't wait to the day before. The same holds for any directional signs you'll be using. Get them out as soon as you can!

With regard to using the Bagua, always place the Open House sign in the Helpful People area, and make sure it is very prominent. Many agents use balloons to draw extra attention to an Open House . . . this is a good idea. I'd prefer you tie three or five balloons on to the mail box, with one of them being a bright yellow and the others being a bright red. These two colors are powerful "attractors", and using one yellow gives off a super contrast which makes people take a look.

Any real estate agent will acknowledge that the more visitors we have, the more potential we have for "making the sale". As a former owner of a real estate company, I was always encouraging the other agents to consider the power of doing an Open House. I always mentioned these reasons for doing one for their homeowner: 1) you please your homeowner who secretly considers it part of doing the job; 2) you may find a potential home buyer to work with; 3) you show people in the neighborhood that you work at your craft; 4) someone may wander in that has a home, and needs to list it; 5) and hopefully you will sell the home that you are holding open. Now that is a lot of great reasons why holding Open Houses on a consistent basis is just good business!

Before Feng Shui came into my life, I had a lot of good come out of using the Open House as a tool. I did sell several of my listings this way, which of course gave me both ends of the commission . . . another super reason. But Feng Shui opened up an entirely new level of success!

I really had gotten quite good at "staging" a home for an Open House, but by using the philosophy of Feng Shui, things just took off. More visitors, more interest, and more offers were the new reality! I thought Open Houses were great before I started staging with Feng shui, and now I can only say that if you aren't doing them . . . you are really wasting an amazing opportunity.

DID YOU KNOW?
Intention is a BIG thing when practicing Black Hat Feng Shui. It is always powerful to visualize a sale of your home everyday. Just picture a SOLD sign out front. Keep this thought always, as if it is already done. Thought, which is another type of energy, does help speed up the process.

My first "Feng Shui" open house was an eye-opener. I had recently sent away for some tapes about the benefits of using something I couldn't even pronounce . . . *Feng Shui*. I started listening immediately, and thought I might pick up some tips for an open house I was running four days later in a vacant house listing I had just picked up. This house had been on the market with another agent for over four months with no offers. It seemed to me that a vacant home was a good place to start practicing this "Feng Shui" stuff!

I borrowed some "props" from my home and attempted to follow the ideas presented on the tapes. At the main entrance I placed an indoor water fountain, in the room to the right . . . the Helpful People area . . . I put my business cards, house brochures, and a multi-colored flower arrangement. The next room, on right side of house moving counter clockwise, was the kitchen, and I placed a white flower arrangement and a bowl of fruit on the island. In the far right back corner. the Relationship area, I put two flowering pink plants, and in the Fame area, I put an ugly fake red flower on top of the fireplace . . . . at the moment it was all I had available. I turned on some soothing classical music, and finally placed two large pots of yellow flowers outside next to the door on the porch. To say I was flabbergasted with the results was an understatement . . . I had very heavy traffic, and TWO offers!!

Coincidence?? Maybe. But as you might imagine . . . *I was hooked!*

Even if you are using Feng Shui, many of the old "Open House" ideas never change. Your homeowner has to be a "partner" in the Open House. The lawn has to be mowed and trimmed. The front door has to sparkle. The house has to smell great . . . with no offensive odors . . . but the norm is NOT enough. You have to go beyond the norm to perform a **Feng Shui Open House.**

The Feng Shui Open House

Many of the ideas that have been presented to you for improving the chances of getting your home sold have to be in place before the Open House. For example: the sense of smell must be activated positively by bringing in cinnamon or French vanilla. These smells need to be consistent throughout the property and not over powering. That means several days before the Open House your home owner needs to begin working with you on this. The sense of feel relates to the temperature. In the summer, the temperature should be no lower than 68 degrees, and no higher than 72 degrees. These temperatures need to be followed in the winter also. A visitor needs to be very comfortable. If they are too cold or too hot, they will leave very quickly and not have good feelings about your house. Your homeowner needs to cooperate; after all they are paying the power bill.

Everything we've discussed about the visual part of getting a home ready using Feng Shui, must be followed also. But for this special day or hours, we will take the process several steps further to make the potential buyer's visit memorable and very powerful.

Even if your Open House is during the day, turn on the outside lights at the front door. Make sure the lanterns at the main entrance, The Mouth of Chi, are sparkling and have been cleaned. Place fresh flowers on both sides of your front door . . . either red or yellow. These flowers have to be *extremely* vibrant and not too small or too high. Make sure they fit the environment. Take away anything at the entrance that does not add to the look, and make sure the "hardware" is glistening. When the buyers walk up to the front door they will be overpowered by how impressive it is. Do NOT compromise here. It must look amazing!

Inside, use candles in groups of three to pull a visitor's attention to particular features. If possible use three varying sizes of pillar candles in the same color in each room. Although you do not need to do this in all rooms, definitely address the den, kitchen, master bedroom, master bath, and one or two other rooms that warrant special attention.

At the start of the Open House, light up three different size candles of one color and place them on the prime area for attention in the kitchen. For example: we can place three blue candles of different heights on the island. This will draw extra attention and energy to this wonderful feature.

In the den, you may choose to use three different size yellow candles placed on the hearth (or mantle) of the fireplace. In the master, we might light three green or pink candles and place them on a table in a bay window. If you have a special bathtub, you may want to show it off by lighting three red candles. Obviously, lighted candles require some safety monitoring during the Open House, and remember to plan for dripping wax.

Homes all have different features that are attractive or unique. Showing them off or "highlighting" them only makes sense, but using lighted candles actually activates other "powers" as well. A candle that is lighted will pull a person's attention toward it, and make the person focus on this feature more intently.

The next sense we need to activate is that of "hearing" or sound. It goes without saying that if the noise coming from inside or outside the house is offensive . . . forget the potential buyers having any real interest! We may have to make sure that traffic or yapping dogs are not as obvious, but even if noise is not a problem, we want to have some soft, pleasant, Yin music playing in the background. We want it to give off the impression to our visitors of **SANCTUARY**. We want to create this "feeling" throughout, and music or sound is a major way of penetrating a person's subconscious.

Offering a snack is another way to activate positive feelings to an open house visitor. Taste, all though coming in fifth in importance, can also help set the mood. I like offering something sweet, like cookies. Sweet is a Yin element, whereas salty items like nuts are more Yang. I want the home to express feelings of comfort and safety, so I like to offer cookies like oatmeal raisin. It is a nice trick to give them something yummy and allow them to take it with them . . . remembering the way they felt in your home.

A **Feng Shui Open House** can be both fun and very productive. It will leave an impression on all of your attendees and probably allow you to "pick up" other listings in the process!

Frequently Asked Questions

Is there one day or time that is better than another for holding an open house?
No. I had signs, both yard and directional, made up for both Saturday and Sunday with the hours of 12 to 2 and 3 to 5. This gave me an hour for travel between houses. I had luck with all of these days and times.

Most of my owners don't like open houses, and neither do I. Isn't this a waste of my time?
PLEASE read this chapter again! I gave you FIVE good reasons that making open houses a habit will help your business. And if you use these new Feng Shui techniques . . . you will never ask a question like this again.

BIBLIOGRAPHY AND FURTHER READING

- *Chic Living with Feng Shui* by Sharon Stasney, Main Street
- *Curb Appeal Idea Book* by Mary Ellen Polson, Taunton
- *The Complete Illustrated Guide to Feng Shui* by Lillian Too, Element
- *The Feng Shui House Book* by Gina Lazenby, Watson Guptill
- *Sell Your Home FASTER with Feng Shui* by Holly Ziegler, Dragon Chi Publications
- *Feng Shui for Dummies* by David Daniel Kennedy, Hungry Minds
- *Living Color* by Sarah Rossbach and Lin Yun, Kodansha America
- *Feng Shui Handbook* by Master Lam Kam Chuen, Owl Books
- *Dress your House for Success* by Martha Webb and Sarah Parsons Zackheim, Three Rivers Press
- *Interior Design with Feng Shui* by Sarah Rossbach, Penguin Compass
- *Feng Shui: a Practical Guide for Architects and Designers* by Vincent M. Smith, Kaplan AEC Education
- *The Western Guide to Feng Shui Room by Room* by Terah Kathryn Collins, Hay House
- *The Tao of Physics* by Fritjof Capra, Shambhala
- *Home Design from the Inside Out* by Robin Lennon, Penguin Arkana
- *Home Staging* by Lori Matzke, Center Stage Home
- *Feng Shui Home* by Gill Hale, Stella Martin, and Josephine De Winter, Barnes and Nobles Books
- *Colors for your Every Mood* by Leatrice Eiseman, Capital Books, Inc.
- *Use What You Have Decorating* by Lauri Ward, Perigee
- *The Declutter Workbook* by Mary Lambert, Sterling
- *Feng Shui in a Weekend* by Simon Brown, Hamlyn

BVG